NO ENCORE!

MUSICIANS REVEAL THEIR WEIRDEST, WILDEST, MOST EMBARRASSING GIGS

DREW FORTUNE

Post Hill
PRESS

A POST HILL PRESS BOOK

No Encore!:
Musicians Reveal Their Weirdest, Wildest, Most Embarrassing Gigs
© 2019 by Drew Fortune
All Rights Reserved

ISBN: 978-1-64293-084-9
ISBN (eBook): 978-1-64293-085-6

Interior design and composition by Greg Johnson, Textbook Perfect
Author photo by Shane Cudahy

This is a work of nonfiction. All people, locations, events, and situations
are portrayed to the best of each contributor's memory.

Post Hill Press
New York • Nashville
posthillpress.com

Published in the United States of America

For Mom and Dad

"It is not the critic who counts, nor the man who points how the strong man stumbled or where the doer of deeds could have done them better. The credit belongs to the man who is actually in the arena; whose face is marred by dust and sweat and blood; who strives valiantly...who knows the great enthusiasms, the great devotions, and spends himself in a worthy cause; who, at best, knows the triumph of high achievement; and who, at the worst, if he fails, at least fails while daring greatly, so that his place shall never be with those cold and timid souls who know neither victory nor defeat."

—THEODORE ROOSEVELT, 1910

"All happy families are alike; each unhappy family is unhappy in its own way."

—TOLSTOY

"The Boston gig has been cancelled. I wouldn't worry about it though. It's not a big college town."

—*THIS IS SPINAL TAP*

CONTENTS

Introduction xiii

1: Alice Cooper. 1

2: Lou Barlow (Dinosaur Jr./Sebadoh). 5

3: Dean Ween (Ween). 10

4: Blothar (formerly Beefcake the Mighty: GWAR lead singer). 14

5: Talib Kweli 19

6: Dave Navarro (Jane's Addiction/Red Hot Chili Peppers) 23

7: Shirley Manson (Garbage) 28

8: The Act of Performance: A short essay by Andrew W.K. 32

9: Zakk Wylde (Ozzy Osbourne/Black Label Society) 35

10: Debbie Gibson 40

11: James Williamson (The Stooges) 44

12: John Bell (Widespread Panic). 50

13: Jane Wiedlin (the Go-Go's). 54

14: Darryl McDaniels (Run-D.M.C.) 57

15: Dee Snider (Twisted Sister). 62

16: Zac Carper (FIDLAR). 67

17: Jared Swilley (Black Lips) 71

18: Nathan Williams (Wavves). 76

19: Terry Ellis (En Vogue) 80

20: Mark Mothersbaugh (DEVO). 84

21: Paul Oakenfold (DJ). 89

22: Peter Frampton. 92

23: Wayne Kramer (MC5) 96

24: King Khan (King Khan and the Shrines, The King Khan
      & BBQ Show, Louder Than Death, The Almighty
      Defend-ers, Tandoori Knights) 99

25: Dave King (Flogging Molly) 108

26: Mike Shinoda (Linkin Park) 113

27: Jennifer Herrema (Royal Trux). 119

28: Big Daddy Kane 125

29: Ian Anderson (Jethro Tull) 130

30: Tunde Adebimpe (TV on the Radio) 135

31: Al Jourgensen (Ministry) 140

32: Robin Wilson (Gin Blossoms). 146

33: Joel Gion (The Brian Jonestown Massacre) 154

34: Courtney Taylor-Taylor (The Dandy Warhols) 158

35: Sean Yseult (White Zombie). 164

36: Sammy Hagar (Van Halen) 169

37: Paul Hartnoll (Orbital) 174

38: Mark Foster (Foster the People). 178

39: Genesis P-Orridge (Throbbing Gristle/Psychic TV). 184

40: David Yow (Jesus Lizard) 192

41: Dave Pirner (Soul Asylum). 197

42: Stephan Jenkins (Third Eye Blind) 201

43: Buzz Osborne (Melvins). 206

44: Chopmaster J (Digital Underground). .212

45: Kenny Loggins. 216

46: Brent Smith (Shinedown) 221

47: Gary LeVox (Rascal Flatts) 225

48: Stewart Copeland (The Police) 230

49: Dan Aykroyd (Blues Brothers) 235

50: Robert Pollard (Guided By Voices) 238

51: MOBY 242

52: Wyclef Jean. 245

53: Brandon Boyd (Incubus) 248

54: Merle Allin (GG Allin and the Murder Junkies) 252

55: Jon Wurster (Superchunk/Bob Mould Band) 258

56: Nick Hexum (311) 266

57: Louis Pérez (Los Lobos) 270

58: Don Brewer (Grand Funk Railroad) 275

59: Lita Ford 279

60: Josh Freese 284

61: Violent J/Shaggy 2 Dope (Insane Clown Posse) 290

Acknowledgments 297

About the Author. 299

INTRODUCTION

In 1997, I flew to Fort Worth, Texas, from Chicago to see my first real concert. It was the Rolling Stones on their Bridges to Babylon Tour—a bloated juggernaut featuring "up-and-comers," including the Dave Matthews Band, the Smashing Pumpkins, and something called Matchbox 20. I was only fifteen but was in a hardcore Stones/Bob Dylan phase. I thought myself a true gourmand, while my peers were swept up in Backstreet Boys and Hanson mania. The show was at the Texas Motor Speedway, an outdoor Mecca of beer and octane, on a hot November day.

After the Smashing Pumpkins limped offstage, berated by liquored-up Texans who were in no mood for openers, Matchbox 20 confidently took the stage. This was before the band's debut *Yourself Or Someone Like You* went on to sell over fifteen million copies and before "3AM" became an MTV staple. They were sitting ducks. I don't remember a thing about the Stones' performance, but I do remember the hatred inflicted upon front man Rob Thomas and company. Cheap beer rained down on my head as overheated Stones fans threw cups, candy, hot dogs, and boxes of popcorn toward the stage, screaming all manner of obscenities at the fledgling band. This next part I swear is true, even through the fog of memory. Rob Thomas stopped the show, gripped the mic, and yelled, "Fuck you! We're gonna be the biggest fucking band in the world!" In 2000, "Bent" hit number one, and Thomas had his revenge. I'm not sure if "Smooth" was an attempt to inflict further torture on the world that had wronged him, but since he declined to participate in this book, I'll never know.

I became a concert junkie that day and spent the better part of my twenties traveling the country seeing shows. Coming of age in the festival era, and with the advent of social media, the disaster concerts, and behind-the-scenes debauchery, continues to have a perverse stranglehold on us. I started this project with the idea of calling it *Rain or Shine*, with the artists recalling their best and worst concerts. Early on, I realized that musicians had no trouble recalling their worst moments and recounted them with a mixture of honor and humor, like a grizzled war vet on open mic night. The best concerts all kind of blurred together: "Well, my family was there, so it was really special." Or, "I had just gotten engaged, so I was really happy that night." It was sweet, but not the reason you watched Mötley Crüe's *Behind the Music* twenty times.

I reached out to my friend Mickey Melchiondo, aka Dean Ween, in 2014, about sharing nightmare gigs for the now revamped project, *No Encore!* He wrote his own chapter, which went mildly viral after he posted it on his blog, and I realized I was on to something. From there, I reached out to the craziest artists I could think of from across the globe for phoners, aiming to make this book as NC-17 as possible. A few artists wrote their own chapters, which has been noted in the text. I also courted artists whose stories I felt like I had never heard, who always fascinated me, or who never made splashy headlines. I wanted to showcase true lifers and those that have overcome addiction, poverty, flameout, and soldiered on. My goal has always been to make this book a celebration of perseverance, the burning desire that keeps artists coming back after experiences that would cause others to hang up their microphones or guitars for a life in music publicity, or, God forbid, music journalism.

So, let's kick out the jams, blow some speakers, and party like we're seventeen again. I love you all.

—Drew

1

ALICE COOPER

Let's face it: This book wouldn't exist without Alice Cooper. The Godfather of shock, Cooper built on the bare bones scare tactics of Screamin' Jay Hawkins and upped the ante with on-stage decapitation, baby doll mutilation, one unlucky chicken, and a python with IBS.

This book is basically about every one of my shows. My show has never been anything but outrageous and crazy. In my fifty years of doing this, with as many theatrics as we have, there's definitely been *Spinal Tap* moments. I've always been setting myself up for those moments. Props just don't work all the time. One time, I had a twenty-foot cannon that would shoot an Alice dummy across the stage into a net. In rehearsal, it worked great. The idea was they would put me in the cannon, and I would get out the back without the crowd seeing it, and the dummy would get shot out the cannon. I think this was at Three Rivers Stadium in Pittsburgh, and the cannon went off on cue. The dummy, however, didn't get shot out, and it just hung there over the edge of the cannon. The audience didn't know if it was a joke, and we decided to play it as a joke. I pulled the dummy out and kicked it. Not my finest moment, but those are the things that can happen.

I guarantee nobody can beat this story. This was in the late '80s, and we were at the House of Blues in Los Angeles. This was on the Alice Cooper Carnival Tour, and I had all the roadies dressed up as psychotic, demented clowns. The Sex Pistols were in the audience, KISS came down for the show, and it was packed. It came time to bring the snake on stage, and I know what kind of reaction the snake gets. This time, everyone was laughing. I was trying to figure it out because no one ever laughs at this point in the show. I suddenly realized that the snake was crapping all over the side of my clothes, and it was the most vile smell you can imagine.

The thing eats dead rats, and it smelled like death. There were piles of snake crap all over the stage. If you can imagine the size of crap that comes from a Great Dane or a small horse, that's what it's like. I'm telling you, there was piles of the stuff. The clowns came out to clean it up, and it was so vile that they started retching and throwing up on the piles of crap. So, now I had a snake that was still crapping all over me, piles of crap on the stage, and a bunch of psychotic clowns were puking into it, making this horrible sludge. We somehow finished the show, and Johnny Rotten came up to me and said, "That was the greatest thing I've ever seen in my life. That was the best theater I've ever seen." Embarrassed, I said, "Yes, we do this every night. I know just where to touch the snake to make him crap." I had to burn my stage costume. I could not get the smell out of it.

The funny thing was that it still worked theatrically. This was before the internet, so I think most of the audience just believed it truly was part of the show. You can't just get vomiting clowns on stage as a regular part of the show. Maybe you can, but that night still stands out for me. That was the only time I ever had a malfunction with the snake. We knew how to handle it. We knew that when it's hungry, the eyes glaze over. They let you know that it's time to feed. The bigger the snake, the longer time it goes between meals. A twelve-foot snake only eats about once a month. We'd give him two or three rats a month, and there was never any danger of it constricting on me.

Snakes are also deaf, so the sound of the show doesn't make them anxious. They're also mostly blind, so the tongue is their smelling apparatus, and it seeks heat. The stage is hot, they feel the vibration of the drums and bass, which doesn't bother them, and they're very happy on stage with that heat. The only thing they react to is adrenaline, which is the same with dogs. If you walk into a yard and a dog starts barking, you don't realize that they're smelling adrenaline. Snakes and dogs smell it, and it immediately puts them on guard. Since I was comfortable with the snake, it wasn't nervous. But if someone picked it up and was scared out of their mind, that would be a different story.

We used to do the "hanging" stunt, with the gallows, and it worked without fail for years. The stunt was that a piano wire came down the back of the rope that the audience doesn't see. I would wear a vest, that connected under my legs, under my stage clothes. That vest absorbed the shock. There was a little tiny loop, so that when they put the rope around my neck, the executioner would thread the piano wire through the loop. The wire was an inch shorter than the rope, so that when it dropped, the rope never really touched my neck. It looked great and like I was really being strangled, but the piano wire stopped it. It worked every night for two years, and we were in London doing a rehearsal. After 200 shows, the piano wire finally snapped, and the rope hit my neck. We all have a survival button in our heads, and my button told me to snap my head back. When I did that, the rope slipped over my chin, rather than leaving me hanging. I hit the floor hard and knocked myself out. The next night, I had piano wire that was three times stronger. The show had to go on.

The stage guillotine is a forty-pound blade that misses my head by six inches every night, and it's razor sharp. Everyone thinks that it's made of Styrofoam or rubber. The only way that you can make the stunt look really good is to make sure that it's as close to my head as possible. Every year, I keep telling the guys to make it closer. Don't try this at home. It's something you have to learn how to do. That's when Doctor Adrenaline kicks in, and that's the secret to my longevity. I need that adrenaline to keep me going. One time I put a sword through my leg. That really would have hurt had it not happened on stage. I knew it went through a muscle, but the adrenaline had kicked in. As soon as the show was over and the adrenaline wore off, I could not stand up. I just poured a bottle of whiskey over the wound because they wanted to give me a tetanus shot, and I wasn't about to go for that at all. I figured it was what James Bond would have done.

Three things are guaranteed, and I tell this to everyone that joins the Alice show. "I guarantee you'll get paid. I guarantee you'll see the world. I guarantee you'll get stitches."

2

LOU BARLOW

(Dinosaur Jr./Sebadoh)

As a founding member of Dinosaur Jr., Lou Barlow made three records with the band before a steady rift with guitarist/vocalist J Mascis turned toxic. Barlow's band Sebadoh, a plaintive, down-tempo project that churned just below the mainstream surface, was deemed ready for the big time in 1994. Remember kids: speed kills.

I have lots of really bad shows, where I freaked out, was too drunk, or stormed off the stage after a couple songs. The most catastrophic show was just after Sebadoh had done the *Bakesale* record. We were kinda popular in England and were slated to play the Reading Festival. We had a pretty good time slot too, sometime around early evening, and we were playing one of the main stages. The record label set up a bunch of stuff for us to do during the day, and one of them was a signing tent. We sat in a little tent on folding chairs, along with the band Pavement. It was a really long line of kids waiting to have their records or whatever signed, and I started drinking. I was drinking huge cans of Stella Artois and probably worked my way through three or four cans, which is a lot with those British tall-boys. We knew Pavement, so we were just laughing and having a good time. Afterwards, I stood up and immediately thought, "Oh...I'm drunk. Shit."

We were set to play in about an hour and a half, and I was stumbling around. I wasn't falling down, but I definitely knew I wasn't close to being at my best, and this was easily going to be the biggest show we'd ever played. There could have been close to 10,000 people at the show. I'm not positive, but it was definitely the biggest. In England, people really pay attention to up-and-coming bands. We were being touted as the new big thing. "Here's your time to shine, Sebadoh! You got the great time slot at the NME Tent. Don't fuck it up!" I was walking around, getting very nervous, and I ran into this guy from one of the festival bands. I'm not going to say his name, but he was a really nice guy. I told him I was feeling a little woozy, and he said, "I got just the thing man."

He suggested we do some speed and that it would straighten me out into a sober-ish realm where I could play decently. I had never done speed. Up to that point, I was strictly a beer and pot guy. I had done coke maybe once or twice, and I had no idea how I would react to speed. We ducked into a tent with his bandmates, who were all super friendly people. He chopped me up, what I now realize, was way too much speed. It was a fuckin' line bigger than my pinky. He gives me this big, fat line, hands me a straw, and says casually, "Here ya go!" I snorted it and thought, "OK! Thanks!" It was a really weird time, as it was shortly after Kurt Cobain died. Sebadoh had been scheduled to tour with Nirvana before Kurt died, and there was this pall hanging over the whole festival. Hole was playing, and Courtney was just on the loose on the festival grounds. Evan Dando was there, and it was prime, mid-nineties, dark, druggy days.

So, I had done way too much speed, but didn't know it yet. I walked on stage, we started the set, and I realized I couldn't even fucking play. My body constricted to the point where I could barely form chords. Sebadoh was a pretty elemental band. It was really simple stuff, and at our best, we just weren't going to deliver on that stage, with a huge crowd. We just weren't a dynamic, technical band at that point. We were this homespun thing, and we had brought along a good friend of ours to drum, but he wasn't really a drummer per se. I was acutely aware of the limitations of the band, because in those festival situations, I would always check out other bands, thinking, "Oh shit, we're still really rinky-dink." At least instrumentally, compared to a lot of what was happening at the time. We lacked that heavy, post-grunge thing, or the intricate Britpop of a band like Blur.

These festivals never brought out confidence in me, so I was already nervous. The tent was packed, the sun had just set, and everything was primed for a normal, great band to kill it. I could barely play, so I broke one of my guitars almost immediately. I just stood there, feeling this hot embarrassment flowing through me. I approached the mic and just started rambling. I told the story of the very first time I played on stage, when I was seven years old. I had learned a few notes on guitar at school, and we had to perform at this little elementary school assembly. I was supposed to pluck out a few notes of, "My Hat, It Has Three Corners." I got so freaked out that in the middle of the thing, which was packed with parents, teachers, and family, I threw my guitar and ran off stage, screaming, "I can't do it!"

On that stage at Reading, that memory was all I could think about. I was recounting this story and how terrible it was, and my bandmates were kind of jamming behind me. Behind me and to my right, Courtney Love was just looming. Suddenly, she started screaming, "You're disrespecting Kurt!" She thought that with me smashing my guitar and having this meltdown on stage, I was somehow disrespecting her late husband. Kurt and I were around the same age, and I was also ambivalent about the idea of fame, but that was it. Then I smashed another guitar, and a piece of it caught the back of my head, so now I'm bleeding, melting down, with Courtney Love yelling at me. I was standing in front of all these people, and the whole tent was just a chasm of silence. I'm still really high and didn't know what to do with myself. Finally, we stumbled through the set, but I don't really remember. There are tapes and streams of this performance, but I can't fucking bear to listen to it.

After the ordeal, I got off stage and met back up with the speed guy. We hung out all night tormenting people. We found out where the guitarist from Ride was hanging out, and we started following him around. We ended up in this hotel room with him and his girlfriend, and they were looking at us like, "Get the fuck out of our room." We were just wandering around on speed with guitars. Later that night, I ended up on a tour bus with Courtney and Evan Dando, who were hanging out together doing really heavy drugs. At some point I barged into the medical tent, screaming, "I'm cut!"

Of course, my injury was completely superficial. In my mind, I was trying to blow the whole show into this monumental, really honest moment.

In retrospect, and certainly within days of the show, I knew that I had really blown it. I've never quite recovered from it. On top of it, I had discovered speed, which gradually became a bigger part of my life—to the point where it ran me into the fucking ground five years later and ruined everything. It's hard to think that on that night, I set in motion something really negative.

3

DEAN WEEN

(Ween)

For over thirty years, Ween has been waving a middle finger at the musical establishment and conventional good taste. Notorious for their early, drug-addled live shows, Dean Ween reveals that playing for a Busta Rhymes crowd is more frightening than a psilocybin-fueled waking nightmare.

Written by Mickey Melchiondo, aka Dean Ween

My Worst Gig Nightmare

We got a gig at the State University of NY (SUNY) on the Plattsburgh campus. Plattsburgh is up on the border of New York and Vermont, so we figured it would be a bunch of hippies in the crowd. What actually happened was that there were two student councils at SUNY Plattsburgh: a black council and a white council. They got to decide the budget for the concert and who they wanted to play at their big Spring Fling event. The black students voted for Busta Rhymes, who was our label mate on Elektra Records at that time. The stoner white kids voted for Ween, and then it was settled. Ween would play before Busta Rhymes in a massive gym that held 5,000 people.

We rented a van for this single show and drove up, all excited. When we got there it was a giant empty room with seemingly no one in charge. Busta Rhymes's posse was there onstage. They had the student sound guy setting up fifty microphones for his boys. They just wandered around the stage and yelled, "make some noise!" There were tough-looking ghetto brothers walking all around the stage and the gym, occasionally yelling into the mics, "Yo, yo, yo. Check one two." Busta Rhymes wasn't even there. The only thing they needed to soundcheck was a turntable and the fifty mics—the easiest soundcheck in the world. Somehow it took three hours. Finally, everybody wandered off, and it was our turn to soundcheck right as the doors were opening. So I wrote a setlist that heavily featured our new songs from *The Mollusk*, which is a very prog-rock record. We go onstage and the whole crowd, as far as I can tell, is black people. We start by playing "The Golden Eel," a song about a fish in Aaron's fish tank that we wrote while tripping on mushrooms.

They hated it. They started throwing cups, bottles, change, chairs, and anything that wasn't nailed down. By the third song, we were dead in the water. I just put my head down and played as best as I could, trying hard to tune out the crowd. All of a sudden, I felt like someone punched me in the stomach with a baseball bat. I got the wind knocked out of me and stumbled backwards. When I looked up there was a forty-ounce bottle at my feet. It had hit me in the gut/dick. The perpetrator was a 300-pound black sister who was standing right below me at my monitor. I looked her right in the eye, and she waved me forward, as if she was going to tell me a secret. I leaned in and she said "Baby, you gots to go." She then stuck two thumbs down in my face to reinforce the point. Then to make sure I heard her, she said again, "Motherfucker, you gots to go!"

We started to make it a challenge; us against the crowd. We can do this with dignity, right? Wrong. By the time we finished our set, it was a game of dodge ball. The whole crowd had a mob mentality and was throwing everything with malicious intent. We were stretching our songs as long as they could go, and I was taking ten-minute guitar solos just to be a dick. For the record, we kicked ass. We were playing with the inspiration of fourteen-year-olds—absolutely fucking shredding to try and win the crowd over to our side. In some sick way I think we did. Anyway, we finish up and find out that Busta Rhymes hasn't even left *Brooklyn* yet! He's three and a half hours away. The teacher rep asks us to go back on, and we laughed in his face as we got our check and left.

That's not the end of the story. We go back to our hotel, which was a Holiday Inn off the side of the interstate. Me and my guitar roadie, Mick Preston, go to the hotel bar and start drinking heavily, trying to forget the whole experience but not really caring so much. We get wasted, and the bar had a pool table that we held for four hours. Around last call, fifty scary looking brothers walk in, and some guy comes over to the pool table and says, "Last game fellas." It was Busta Rhymes and his posse. I tell the guy that if Busta wants to shoot pool, he has to beat us first, and I also want to tell him a story. So Busta Rhymes walks over to the pool table, and I introduce myself and tell him the story about what it was like opening up for him. After all, we are on the same record label, and we both have new records out. Well, he thought it was the funniest story he ever heard, me getting hit with bottles and everything. He said, "This is Mickey from the Ween; they're not very popular with the brothers!" He made me re-tell the story of our gig to every guy in his crew and posse, and they were laughing their asses off.

He paid for the drinks for the rest of the night, and me and Mick played doubles against him and his bodyguard on the pool table until like 5:00 a.m. I think he gave the bartender $5,000 to keep the bar open just for us. He was the nicest guy in the world. He kept high-fiving me and had me tell him the story of the gig over and over until I was hoarse. He bought all the champagne in the place; Moet, White Star—the best they had. It wasn't Cristal, but Moet is pretty delicious. That's pretty much the end of the story. We all stumbled back to our rooms, and I distinctly remember him giving me a hug and telling me we'd see each other again out there, but it never happened and probably never will again.

4

BLOTHAR

(formerly Beefcake the Mighty: GWAR lead singer)

My first internship was at the House of Blues in Chicago in 2004. Walking in one day, I saw one of the show bookers with his head hung low. I asked what was wrong, and he said, "We just booked GWAR. Fuck."

The craziest gig that we've played was City Gardens with Murphy's Law back in the late '80s, and all of these skinheads showed up. They had their nice, polished swastika jackets on, and there we were on stage, spraying blood all over the place. As soon as we sprayed blood on their jackets, they just lost their minds and attacked the band. They did this thing called the "Wall of Death," which was this thing they would do if they hated a band. They would clear everyone from the floor and rush the stage. There was a steel barrier between us and the skinheads, but they pushed everyone to the side of the venue. Once they had everyone shoved out of the way, they went to the back of the club and ran full-speed towards the stage. They were trying to get enough speed to hop over that barricade. Security was present, but it was the old days, and they weren't really doing jack shit.

At the time, we had this piece of equipment called the "Spew Chandelier." It was a chandelier that spewed blood on the crowd, but because of the way it was designed—*poorly*—it sprayed blood backwards too. This may have been the only show that we used the fucking thing, and the Sexecutioner, our bandmate Chuck Varga, noticed that some of the skinheads were slipping on the floor. Chuck took the hoses out of the Spew Chandelier and started spraying the floor with the fake blood. When the skinheads got close to the stage, they all started falling down. It was like watching the Keystone Kops...they were falling all over the place and wriggling around. After that, their attack pretty much fizzled out. We all thought it was hilarious.

Back in the early days of GWAR, we had a lot of weird shows. The weirdest was this tiny little room in Bielefeld, Germany called AJZ. This was the first time we'd ever played there, and the audience didn't know anything about us. The entire crowd was made up of these politically conscious, straight-edge punk rockers. Once we got on stage and started playing and spraying shit, they all ran away to the back of the room. They were terrified of getting sprayed, and we figured that once the shock wore off, they'd come forward and start liking it. But that never happened. They stayed pinned to the back of the club the entire show. When we got off stage after the show, they started questioning us. I'll never forget the line of questioning, which was basically, "Why do you do this? What are you trying to achieve?" We didn't really know how to answer. We were like, "Because we're fucking GWAR, and we spray people with shit! That's what we do!"

The most trouble we ever got in at a show was when our lead singer Dave Brockie (Oderus Urungus) got arrested. He's no longer with us, and it happened at a show in North Carolina back in the early '90s. Brockie was Canadian, so he had to cop a plea to this. Otherwise, he would have been labeled a sex offender and would have had to leave the country. What happened was we were playing this show in Charlotte, and I look out to the back of the crowd and see this line of uniformed policemen. I figured a fight or something was going on. Suddenly, I noticed this group of guys in cheap dress pants and ties lining the stage. They were fucking detectives, but we didn't know it at the time. They started motioning to us to come off the stage. Their attitude was, "Hey! This is over. Get off the damn stage!" They walked on stage, with all the blood and shit spraying all over the place. We thought maybe it was just over-zealous security, so started yelling, "Get the fuck outta here" while pushing them down.

That's when they started flashing their badges and guns. We immediately were like, "Oh! OK officers!" By that point, they were amped. They thought they were gonna have to fight us. We weren't trying to fight them, we just didn't know who they were. The show stopped, we went off stage, and the crowd was going fucking crazy, booing and throwing shit. Backstage, they told Oderus to take off his mask and shoulder pads. The one thing they made clear to him was, "Leave the big, fake dick on." They made him remove his entire costume, except for the big, fake penis. I distinctly remember yelling, "Wait, fuck that! Don't do it." They were trying to make it seem like that was all he was wearing on stage—just a big, fake dick that wasn't attached to a costumed monster. They yelled at me to, "Shut the fuck up," so I did. I was only twenty years old at the time.

I shut up, and they took all of these pictures of Brockie wearing the fake dick. Then, they put on rubber gloves and put the penis in a five-gallon bucket. They sealed it up, took our prop, and disappeared. We had no idea what to do. Eventually, the promoter and Brockie were arrested. Dave had to be arraigned and was set to appear before a judge. It's ridiculous that this is true, but it is. The judge was named Richard Boner. I swear to God. He was pronouncing it like "Bonner" but c'mon. On the day of Brockie's trial, there was a family of little people who had been in some kind of domestic dispute. It was a husband, wife, and their kids, who were all small. Then, there was us and the fake dick. You couldn't make this shit up.

Brockie was on the stand, and they lifted the "Cuttlefish of Cthulu" (which was what we called the dick) out of the bucket and presented it to the court. They started reading the charges, which were: "He was wearing this on stage. He simulated sex with a dog. He was eating feces and his own vomit." The entire courtroom was aghast. They were reading this stuff like it had really happened and wasn't just part of a normal GWAR show. There was no context. At the time, the principal figure in North Carolina was Senator Jesse Helms, who was extremely conservative. Charlotte was very politically backwards at the time, so they were trying to make an example out of us for obscenity and whatever else. The best part was that with all that went down, we didn't miss any show dates! We grabbed Brockie straight from the courtroom, split, and kept right on touring.

5

TALIB KWELI

One of my regrets with this book is that I wasn't able to get more hip-hop artists to share. It wasn't for lack of trying, and I wasn't about to pay Luther Campbell from 2 Live Crew his interview fee of $3,000. I'm thankful that Talib was so open about the problems hip-hop artists face from venues who don't respect the craft.

My absolute worst gig was in North Carolina, a long time ago at the start of my career. I was staying at a hotel that was really far away from the venue, and I couldn't find a cab service. Meanwhile, I was running really late, the crowd at the venue were getting anxious, and I'm steady trying to find a damn taxi. When I got one and finally pulled up to the venue, a fan came up to me really irate. This dude was spitting and yelling in my face. I had a road manager at the time who was a very aggressive type, and he grabbed this guy by the neck and pushed him away from me. That person's friend came up to me, acting like he was a fan, and punched me right in my face. So now, me and my road manager are fighting with these guys outside the venue, and we got separated. The people we were fighting with ran into the show.

I went onstage, all disheveled and bloody. I said into the mic, "I'm not performing, because I was just attacked." I saw the guy in the audience while I was talking, and I jumped into the crowd to try and get at him. The crowd, not understanding what was going on, wouldn't let me. It turned into a situation where we either had to perform or not get paid. I performed, even though I definitely didn't want to. In the ensuing chaos, I ended up not getting paid anyway. I had blood pouring out from the top of my head for my troubles. Because of that incident, I got wise really quick. The idea that I would do a show because I had to get paid, even though I didn't want to, is something I never did again.

I tour and perform more than any other hip-hop artist. Touring and performing is my life's blood. The stage is my life. As a performer, everything I do is preparation for me hitting that stage. When I'm onstage, that's real. Everything else is just leading up to that moment. As a professional, I've learned how to drink responsibly and to exercise. I grew up smoking weed but not drinking alcohol. I did develop alcoholic tendencies over time, but that didn't happen until after I became a professional rapper. I consider myself a working-class MC. Working-class people drink a lot. People who have to constantly work need a few beers, a couple glasses of wine, or a few whiskeys on the daily.

As a species, we self-medicate. As I've gotten older, it's taken a toll on my body. I can't do it as much as I used to when I was younger. The key was knowing my body well enough to know when to stop. I don't trust a man that doesn't have vices. I wrote a song called "Get By," which is that responsibility of knowing your limit. My vices of choice are alcohol and weed, and I used to get drunk and high before shows a lot back in the day. There were years where I didn't do a sober show. You didn't see me onstage without a drink. I had one show in Amsterdam at the start of my career with Mos Def that, in my mind, I remembered as being excellent. I remember it sounding great and having an amazing time. But then I remembered the look from everybody on my team as I finished, that was like, "What was that?" The look from El-P and Mos Def read, "You look high."

To be a rock artist, you have to study musicality a little bit. Punk rock is kids who pick up instruments without any training. Punk rock is the closest thing to hip-hop in the rock world. Hip-hop comes from city, after-school, and music programs being cut. That's where the disco era came from. The rise of the DJ came from New York City music programs getting cut. People stopped being interested in what instrument you played or hiring bands for their parties. The DJs were cheaper, and kids were growing up not knowing musicality. Hip-hop has never been dependent on knowing an instrument. You literally can get up and rap a cappella or rap over an existing record.

Because the skill of hip-hop isn't centered around the instrumentation, hip-hop artists don't require as much equipment. Sometimes the people responsible for presenting hip-hop shows, or the promoters who don't respect hip-hop, can be lazy. The sound man might be a rock guy who has been working at the same club for years, and a rapper comes up and says, "I'm just gonna rap over this CD." A lot of times, the sound guy doesn't respect that. I've had run-ins with sound guys who don't look at hip-hop as music. I think that with a rock show, there's the potential for a lot more things to go wrong. There's so many pieces that make up a rock show. There's a lot of hip-hop acts that use instruments at this point in history. What's great about traditional hip-hop—the two turntables and a microphone—is that the rapper can go a cappella if the record skips, and that's part of the skill of hip-hop.

Sound guys and venue owners not respecting hip-hop is an all-too-familiar occurrence. I had a big blowout with a sound guy on my birthday in 2015. It was at a classic Boston club called The Middle East. I was talking to the sound man during my set, trying to get the levels right. The sound guy did something I consider highly disrespectful. He got on the microphone so everyone in the room could hear and challenged the notes I was giving him. I wasn't asking for his feedback. This was not a democracy. If anything, he should have relayed a message to my tour manager. I spoke to him and told him that he needed to get the shit right.

The guy came onstage and started trying to argue with me about the sound during the show. Later, I learned the guy had been at the club for thirty years. He thought he had the right to say, "Who's this fucking punk challenging me in my club?" I got on the mic and said, "The show is over until this guy is removed from the building." I left and went into the dressing room. The venue owner came backstage three minutes later, saying, "I apologize for that. I've made him go home." Once he said the guy had gone home, I immediately got back on stage, and the show continued. The next day, the sound guy got on Twitter and challenged me to an MMA bout. He wrote some shit challenging me to get in the Octagon for a fight. I clowned him on Twitter all day, and that was the last I heard from Mr. Sound Man.

6

DAVE NAVARRO

(Jane's Addiction/Red Hot Chili Peppers)

Before becoming a reality TV gadfly, Dave Navarro was alternative excess personified. From his early years as guitarist in Jane's Addiction and Porno for Pyros, through a short stint in Red Hot Chili Peppers, Navarro was the elegantly wasted, darkly sexual pin-up for the doom generation, with a penchant for heroin syringe art.

You'll have to forgive me, because my memory of the drug days is a little blurry. Back in 1997, Jane's Addiction was on tour, and we were playing the KROQ Almost Acoustic Christmas show. It was at the Universal Amphitheater, and it was the height of my drug addiction. I was shooting up heroin and cocaine on a daily basis. I've done tons of tours completely sober since, but back then, I was really, really deep in it. That entire tour, I was pretty out of my mind. I was somehow able not fall down on stage, but before or after, or sometimes during, I was shooting. I was legitimately the member who couldn't be found. Nobody knew where I was. I would shoot a ton of coke, then do the heroin to come down. Or, I would speedball, so I had an option. [*Laughs*]

I could be really up or down. The thing about shooting cocaine is there's a big rush and then it wears off relatively quickly, so you end up shooting a lot. With the speedball, one shot will get you through a couple hours easily. There were many times during the 1997 tour where I had five or six syringes set up and ready to go off the side of the stage. In between songs, I would reapply. It was no secret to the band members, but I don't think the audience was aware. I'd wait for Perry [Farrell] to talk to the audience, or a change in the production, to duck behind the guitar tech and gear station to fix. I'd only get a few minutes, and I hate to say it, but I got really good at doing it quickly.

Anyway, back to the Acoustic Christmas show. For shows like that, there's a number of different artists playing, which is usually somewhere around ten bands. Fiona Apple was playing, and she was breaking as a huge act. It was the height of Fiona mania. I was a fan, and I also had this distant crush on her. I had never met her, but I was really psyched to be playing the same bill with her. I got to the venue early for sound check, and with multiple bands on the bill, you sound check and then wait around all day. What's a junkie gonna do all day long but shoot coke and heroin? The process of shooting up involves inserting the needle into the vein, and pulling back a little bit on the plunger to make sure you've hit the vein. A little blood rushes into the syringe, and then you know you're good. If you miss the vein, you're gonna run into problems and really injure yourself.

I developed a system where I would extract blood without anything in the syringe. I'd spike the vein, and pull out a syringe full
of blood, which led to loads of fun over the years. [*Laughs*] In the
midst of my insanity, I thought it would be a very romantic gesture
to go into Fiona Apple's dressing room, and write a message on her
wall in my own blood. In my deranged head, I viewed it as sending her a message with the blood that pumps through my heart to
her. It was my life blood that I was symbolically sharing. I thought
we would relate on multiple levels because we're both passionate
musicians and artists. In my head, it was a grand, romantic state-
ment that she would find very touching.

She hadn't arrived at the venue yet, so I snuck into her dressing room and began to extract blood out of my arm. With the
syringe, you can aim it and basically paint with it. You can write
words, and it was a technique that I had perfected over the years.
There was no innuendo or poetry in the message I wrote her. It just
read, "Dear Fiona, I hope you have a great time tonight. Love Dave."
That was it. It wasn't too over the top. In my coke-addled brain, it
was a very subtle, kind, romantic gesture. I saw us riding off into
the sunset, with this gesture being the basis for our romance. As
it turned out, the management and staff at the Universal Amphitheater didn't see it that way.

The next thing I know, my manager comes into my dressing
room, asking, "Did you go into Fiona Apple's dressing room?" I
said, "Yeah!" I was proud of it. I continued, "Of course I did! I left
her a little message, wishing her luck on the gig." I tried explaining
that there was no better way to express my sincerity to her than
with the blood that runs through my veins. About five minutes

later, I was in a meeting with staff and management. I'm not sure if her management was involved or if she even saw the message, because an hour later, a team of crime scene cleanup people in hazmat suits began disinfecting her room. Instead of thinking that I was in some kind of trouble or that I made a horrible mistake, I was gutted that my loving gesture had been evaporated from the planet. In my drugged-out state, I couldn't comprehend that a message written in syringe blood—from someone she had never met—might have been frightening. Had someone come into my dressing room and written a message in blood to me, I would have thought it was incredible. That's how sick I was.

Around that same time, I was hanging out at Marilyn Manson's house a lot. I would shoot up in his bathroom, and I would do the same thing. I would spray the bathroom mirror with blood. He was so freaked out by it that he called his housekeepers and assistants to clean it off. I remember thinking that this guy was the king of scary-rock-horror goths. Why is he so freaked out by a little blood? His reaction was so funny that, naturally, I did it again. [*Laughs*] This time around, I thought, "C'mon Mr. Scary! You can't handle a little blood?" I really painted his mirror that time, and he did not appreciate it. My thinking was that if the first two times didn't go over well, the third time would work. After the third time, I began to realize: people don't dig this.

It wasn't until years later, when I met my future wife Carmen Electra, that someone finally liked my syringe art. We were in a hotel room, and I sprayed a heart on the bathroom ceiling. She thought it was the most beautiful, touching gesture in the world. So, the whole thing ended up with a happy ending. The whole thing was just organic art to me. These stories weren't embarrassing to me at the time because of the state I was in. When I got clean and reflected, I couldn't believe I had fucking done it. I got sober somewhere in the early 2000s, but it's an ongoing process. I've definitely struggled with it, but for the most part, I've kept it together. I have a very happy and productive life and feel blessed to have been forgiven for my behavior. It's certainly not a version of myself that I ever want to revisit. The moral of the story is to make sure you only spray blood for the person you're going to marry.

7

SHIRLEY MANSON

(Garbage)

A stylistic and empowerment icon for over two decades, Shirley Manson will always be the coolest woman in the room, even if she's not always the most coordinated performer. It was also really charming to hear her say, "Poo" in her Scottish accent.

I feel that every time I step on stage, something embarrassing, or deeply shameful, is bound to occur. This story has stayed with me and is burned deeply into my memory bank. Garbage had just played our biggest gig ever, at Wembley in London, the night before. It was a huge success, and my idol, Chrissie Hynde, was there. It was my rock 'n' roll fantasy, when everything came together perfectly—my career was skyrocketing, and we were number one all over the place. I felt like Whitney Houston in *The Bodyguard*. It was fucking mental! After the gig, we got on the bus and woke up the following day in Bingen, Germany. We were late to the gig, so we didn't have a sound check or get to see the stage. We were immediately rushed to the backstage facilities, which consisted of a few ropes, tarps, and a makeshift tent for the gents in the band. They put me in a small caravan that was missing its back wheels, so it was at a slanted angle. Every time I tried to move about, I fell. We were still so pumped from playing Wembley that we didn't really care.

The guys ran up these little steps to get on stage with great excitement, and everything seemed to be going just great. I come on stage a little after the band because they have to get their instruments on. When I finally ran out—to my abject horror—I realized we were playing this tiny stage that overlooked the ruins of a small castle. There was a little pit in front of the stage, which was basically a little grassy knoll, with a smattering of German adults and a handful of children. They were all munching on picnics and had thermoses. It was still daylight, as it takes forever for the sun to go down in Germany at that time of year. There was something so funny about the way the guys bounded on stage, as if we were playing Madison Square Garden, to play to about thirty—maximum—picnicking German families.

We opened with the song, "Temptation Waits," and I just got the giggles. I literally couldn't fucking stop. I couldn't sing a single word. I laughed for the duration of the whole fucking song. It was so awful and embarrassing, but I just couldn't get myself together.

After the show, I came off stage and immediately needed to poo. There were no backstage facilities, so I had no idea what to do. I ended up squatting and pooping in a cup in my broken caravan. Afterward, I stood there holding the damn cup and couldn't find anywhere to throw it. I poked my head out of the caravan and decided that the only thing to do was throw it over a wall that led to a dead drop into the countryside. On the way to the wall with my poo cup, I bumped into our tour manager, who was coming to collect my in-ear monitor. I was hiding the cup behind my back and acting all shifty. I managed to get the poo over the wall, and I went back to my cursed caravan. It was an incredible juxtaposition between the greatest gig of our career to one of the most humbling, and saddest.

I'm not a person who gets embarrassed, but here's one where everyone was embarrassed for me. We were playing the KROQ Weenie Roast show in 2016, which is a big summer festival. We hadn't played in a while, and I was really focused on trying to remember lyrics and cues. In the throes of all this, I failed to realize that we were set up on a circular, revolving platform. There was a step down to the stage proper and then the audience in front of me. I was singing "Special," and I took a step onto the lip of the revolving platform, and I stumbled down onto the stage, falling off the stage into the crowd. There was a girl in the front row, and I can remember her face as I was falling into her, which was a shrieking mask of horror.

I fucked myself up pretty bad, but I didn't miss a beat. You can watch the video on YouTube. I kept right on singing and didn't lose my place. I've been doing this for thirty years, and that was my first fall on stage. Everybody was completely mortified. Our social media feeds were flooded with messages saying, "Don't feel too embarrassed, Shirley!" Up until that point, I hadn't really felt embarrassed. If I was more proper, I might have burned with more shame. I'm just glad I didn't break my fucking neck.

One time I lost my wedding ring. I'd been married for two weeks, and we were playing a show in New Zealand. Someone in the audience grabbed my hand, and I noticed my ring was missing. I was freaked and sang an entire song without my wedding ring. Right after the song ended, I screamed into the mic, "Whoever's got my fucking wedding ring better give it back right the fuck now!" Slowly, this very shaky hand reached out to the stage from the audience with the ring. I don't think it was intentional, just opportunism. I can't blame anyone for that. I'm not sure these are the kinds of stories you were looking for. I'm sure you wanted something much more outrageous, where I sucked a man off on stage and spat his cum all over the audience. Sorry to disappoint.

THE ACT OF PERFORMANCE

A short essay by Andrew W.K.

I was pretty confused when I couldn't get a single crazy, embarrassing, or fucked-up gig out of W.K. He kept insisting that he couldn't remember any, and I didn't realize until later that he can be notoriously cryptic in interviews. Regardless, here's a chapter about always striving to be a better performer, with W.K. in full motivational mode.

As a performer, almost every show seems like the worst for me. Conversely, almost every show feels like the best in a strange way. An unfortunate aspect of my experience as a performer is that it's very rare, in a beautiful way, to feel that a show went perfect. I never complete an experience on stage and feel that there's nothing that I could have done better. Learning to accept that feeling is a big rite of passage, as you have to learn and accept that perfection is not what performance is about. It's not about me feeling like I had a perfect show. Sometimes the shows I think are the worst from my perspective will be the best for someone in the band or for an audience member.

If I ask what made it so special for them, usually it was something that was completely out of my control. That's what makes performing such a mysterious and elusive craft. There's only so much ability I have, for better or worse, to control what goes on once I hit the stage. My mindset now is that I'm not allowed to have a bad show. A truly consummate, professional performer—and I don't know if I'll ever get there in this lifetime—has no bad shows. A great performer, and a real mature performer of any age, only has great or amazing shows. There should never be that feeling that anything they have done could have been improved in any way, and that's a great show. An amazing show is when everything goes wrong, and they still put on a great show.

That's something I aspire to, which is to never crack and to never give in to emotions like frustration. The performer should never let themselves stand in the way of the show. My feeling, nine times out of ten, is pure sadness after a show. It's not sadness as a rational emotion but sadness as a physical emotion. The feeling has all the trappings, surroundings, and textures of sadness, without that core interior truth that would justify true sadness. I feel sad for no reason after most of the shows, and I'm trying to accept that feeling as a physical reaction, which is the recovery of endocrine and serotonin levels balancing back out.

On this current tour, there have been a few shows where I felt amazing afterward. That was so rare in the past. I finally felt like I couldn't have done any better and didn't have that sadness. On the other hand, those are shows that fans could have felt were the worst. It's baffling, in a very humbling way. There are also people who just don't understand what I'm trying to do. I encounter that at festivals, when people just pass by and stop to check us out. The music is what empowers me with that energy, that aggressive, "party-starting" mentality. I've played shows early on, for four or five people who definitely didn't like what I was doing, probably for good reason. But, there's maybe one person that did like it, and that would lead to another opportunity.

Most people truly do not like what I do. At this point, anyone that shows up after this many years, there's an understanding that they really want to be there. They do connect with it, and that's hugely meaningful to me. I feel like it's a special team of people who found each other, or found this feeling, that we're all inter-ested in and able to conjure up together. That feeling has become more precious to me. It's so easy to become disconnected these days. Those pinpoints of connection, those bright yet very fragile lights of understanding, go a long way.

9

ZAKK WYLDE

(Ozzy Osbourne/Black Label Society)

(Bobbi Bush: If you're reading this, please get in touch. I really want to know what Zakk was like in high school and how bad the fallout was from your party. #epic)

Before the craziness of Ozzy and Black Label, I was in a high school band called Stonehenge, back in Jackson, New Jersey. We were all about seventeen, and we went to school with a girl named Bobbi Bush, whose family was moving. We'd mostly play keg or basement parties, but this Bobbi Bush gig was legendary. Her house was already sold, and her parents had left for the weekend. She invited all her friends from school, but half the town showed up to trash the place. All the furniture was gone, so we set up in the living room. The house was still livable, with maybe the dining room set and beds intact, but they were on their way out, with the new owners set to take over within a week. I have no idea what the parents were thinking, going off to the Poconos and leaving their daughter in an empty house that was begging to be annihilated by Jersey metalheads.

It's always great when it ain't your house, and it turned into something out of the movie *Weird Science*, where all the mutants on motorcycles crash the place. It was every parent's nightmare, and as a homeowner now I think, "Are you fucking kidding me?" It was a bi-level house, and the whole fucking thing was packed to the gills. To top it off, there was a torrential downpour that night, to the point where my feet sunk while walking across the lawn. Every asshole was dragging mud into the place and ruining the carpets. People were putting their cigarettes out on the carpeting, spilling beer everywhere, and smashing holes in the walls. We opened the show with "Bark at the Moon." Here I am all these years later, closing out shows with Ozzy playing that tune.

Bobbi's parents came home early, just as we were loading up the gear in my buddy Tommy's truck to leave. The mud was so bad we had to prop it up with two-by-fours to get the hell out of there. Between the kegs, hard alcohol, marijuana, and the Caligula factor of people having sex in the bedrooms, the house should have been condemned. Her parents walked in and, aside from some drunk stragglers, we were the only people left. We didn't say a thing and basically ran out the door. I will never forget the look on her parents' faces. Anger hadn't registered yet. They were just gray. The last thing I saw on my way out was "Stonehenge Was Here," tagged on the living room wall in green spray paint. The million-dollar question we all had was, "What happened to Bobbi Bush?" They moved shortly after, and I never saw her again.

This was one of the craziest Ozzy gigs. After the tragic death of Randy Rhoads, Ozzy got word that people were vandalizing Randy's grave. To me, it's one of the most sacrilegious things you can do. If I was a fan of the guy, the last thing I'd want to do is fuck with his grave. I'd be waiting for a lightning bolt to hit me in the graveyard. It was typical silly shit, like how people mess with Hendrix or Jim Morrison's grave. Randy's mom and Ozzy decided to play a gig to raise money to build Randy a mausoleum so people would stop fucking with his grave.

I was pretty new to the band. Halfway through the benefit show, we were about to play "Crazy Train." Oz yelled, "Who wants to go extra crazy?! Come up on stage and dance with the Oz!" We broke into the song and, sure enough, everyone rushed the stage. The barriers crashed down and crazed fans started climbing onstage. Security was like, "Oh, fuck this," and ran off. It was a sea of bodies, with about 200 people onstage with us. It quickly devolved into chaos, with people trying to take microphones and monitors, and ripping the drum set apart. We almost got to the guitar solo, but that was it. Kids were climbing the huge projection screens we had set up behind us. The weight of the bodies caused one of the screens to snap and people came flying down. I know one guy broke his leg.

Ozzy had buckets of water onstage that he would throw into the crowd. Those all got spilled, and the water rushed over the monitor console, causing smoke and sparks to fly everywhere. It was mass insanity. I wasn't scared. If someone wants to mess with me, I'll break their fucking neck. I was just in awe of the whole goddamn thing. Ozzy had a sixty-inch teleprompter with the song lyrics, and that got stolen, along with microphones, snare drums, and cymbals. Our drummer at the time, Randy Castillo, was stabbing people in the fucking neck with his drumstick. The damages to the venue, along with broken bones, was something like two hundred grand. We still got Randy the mausoleum, but the damage bill was fucking ridiculous.

I was standing right next to Ozzy during "Crazy Train." Right when Ozzy goes, "Things are going wrong for me," someone tried to steal the microphone. They were trying to pry it right out of his hands, and they eventually got it. Right before my guitar solo, Randy stopped playing, then I stopped. Ozzy gave me a look like, "Do you fucking believe this?" Ozzy has studied a ton of Jeet Kune Do, just like Elvis did during his karate phase. Ozzy studied with Dan Inosanto, who was one of Bruce Lee's best buddies. Oz probably knocked out about five people that night before we left.

I had a legendary, Hall-of-Fame, world-championship relationship with drinking before I quit. Between neck, back, and shoulder surgeries, I was like a banged-up car that didn't run anymore. We were out on the road with Static-X and Mudvayne in 2009, and I noticed that the back of my leg was killing me right below the knee. I thought it was from the David Lee Roth splits I was doing at the Shoot 'n Stab bar the night before. During the "Animal House" years of Black Label, it wasn't just the band partying—it was the driver, crew, and anybody who wanted to come out.

One night on Ozzfest, my wife called and said, "The Berserker has got to stop. I'm shutting him down." I said to my immortal beloved, "Why, what's the matter?" She asked if I had seen the credit card bill. Every day, me and a few of the fellas went to the liquor store, without fail. We would come out with a palette of booze, and we weren't getting the cheap shit. It was top shelf or whatever local microbrew was available—we tried it all. That was our daily routine, so when my wife called about it, I braced myself. "How bad is the tab?" I asked her. She told me to take a guess. I grumbled and said, "Ten grand?" There was dead silence on the other end of the phone. "Fifteen?" Silence. "Twenty?" She told me to guess again. I said, "OK. Twenty-five grand?" More silence. Now I was getting worried. I said, "It can't be more than thirty-five!" She said, "Keep going." The total was $51,000. On booze alone. In less than a month.

My leg was still hurting, so I went to the doctor with my wife. He told me I had a blood clot behind my knee, one in the calf, and one going into my Achilles Heel. I thought only older people got blood clots, but he told me a lot of it comes from being stationary. I realized that except for the stage, I was on a bus or parked in a bar drinking. The doctor finally said, "With all your years of heavy drinking, the alcohol thinning your blood may have saved your life." I raised my arms in victory and yelled, "See! Drinking is good for something!" There was no laughter from anyone else.

That was the end of the road for me and booze. I stopped cold turkey and became the fucking designated driver. There was a lot more laughter than dark times with it. No matter how banged up I was the night before, I never missed a gig. But, I had to drink about four beers just to feel normal in the morning. That was it, and the booze wasn't why I grew up with Hendrix and Page posters on my wall. I got to the big leagues and get to play with the Yankees. I never let myself forget that. I'm fucking blessed and wouldn't change my situation for anything.

10

DEBBIE GIBSON

I bet you never thought you'd read a book with Debbie Gibson and Zakk Wylde! Thankfully, you know me. As you'll read, Debbie was kinda punk rock, sneaking into twenty-one-plus venues when she was only sixteen, while winning over drag queens and LA's seedier underbelly.

I'm really lucky because I haven't had too many "Oh my God, I'm quitting showbiz" moments in my long career. I grew up in theater and learned very early that something going wrong onstage is an opportunity. It's an opportunity to use humor and to give the audience a once-in-a-lifetime experience because that's what live shows are meant to be anyway. The first nine months of club gigs prepared me for the rest of my career. I've had piano lids get stuck on stage. My dancers lifted my head right through a stucco ceiling during "Fallen Angel." Ashlee Simpson didn't have those nine months, and that awkward jig on *Saturday Night Live* is an example of how not to react.

I started as a "track" artist at the age of sixteen because my first single, "Only In My Dreams," was a dance song. I always hated that there was no flexibility with that term, as I was always locked into the same twenty-five-minute show, three times a night, four nights a week. That's what I did for nine months to get that single off the ground. I was sixteen, and my mom was managing me. I was never the type to sneak into clubs or steal my sister's ID because I was super focused on my work. I wasn't a high school party girl, so it was very funny and ironic that I ended up promoting my single in twenty-one-and-over clubs.

In one night, I would play teen, straight, and gay clubs. It was clubs in East LA with armed men escorting us in. Nobody could peg my age, and it was before Tiffany and I could use our age as a gimmick or advantage. My label had no idea what to do with a sixteen-year-old, so we had to really work it on the club circuit. After the show, my mom would say, "Kids, wait in the car. I'm gonna go collect the money from the promoter. If I'm not back in fifteen minutes, someone come get me." It was really gritty, as she was collecting money from drag queens and mafioso club owners. Sometimes a shooting had just occurred, and we were the last act before they were shutting the club down. It was nuts, but where I developed my love for the LGBTQ community. I remember playing a lesbian club in Brooklyn when I was sixteen and a bunch of sweaty lesbians hugging and kissing me. I thought they were so cool.

My night would start around 9:00 p.m. and end around 6:00 a.m. I would do my twenty-five-minute set, change in the car, and move on to the next club, with my mom driving. I had my two young, gay, male backup dancers with me, and we were a very naive, innocent group. Buddy Casimano is still one of my dancers. We went to high school together, and he's danced with me at my first track show at Joey's Place in Clifton, New Jersey, all the way to Rock in Rio for 150,000 people, and everything in-between. So, it was my two boys, my mom, and my twenty-one-year-old sister Karen, who was on sound and lights, all packed into a car.

Back then, I always sang live, but my backing tracks were on reel-to-reel tape. Karen was always met with a lot of resistance from the DJs at the time, as it was such a male world. She would crawl into these little DJ booths and mix my sound. One night, Karen climbed a ladder up to this DJ booth, and the DJ said, "Listen, Little Miss Sound Engineer, you're not touching my equipment." She tried to explain that she needed to set up the reel-to-reel, but he just grabbed the tape from her and proceeded to put them on backwards.

The show started, and I came out to this garbled, backward-sounding mess. I looked at Karen, who just shrugged. I thought to myself that this crowd is so drunk, and they don't give a shit about me, so why not perform anyway? I sang the whole twenty-five-minute show over horrendous, backward tape. It sounded like a record playing backward, but there was still a groove. I cued my voice and eventually got the crowd clapping. I'll never forget that night because, right after, I went to my junior prom. But, that's a whole other story.

When grunge hit like a wrecking ball in the '90s, I credit theater for not sending me into depression. I had always wanted to do Broadway, so the minute grunge hit, I was pretty rational and realistic, even though there was a tremendous backlash against me and my kind of pop music. I remember MTV telling me that they were not going to air the "Electric Youth" video anymore because there was so much backlash. The people I thought were my friends were easy come, easy go. So, I went right into *Les Misérables* on Broadway and always kept in mind that things are cyclical. I did have to work the carnival/pig wrestling events for years. I ran into Mark McGrath from Sugar Ray a few years ago, and we joked about that time. We call it the "funnel cake years." I really enjoyed that time, and since I've been doing this for so long, I enjoy the whole weird, rollercoaster of it all.

For the last five years, I've been dealing with Lyme Disease, which has brought on so many changes to my body and voice. I used to feel like Superwoman when I was performing, and I can't do that anymore. The options have been to cancel or to get out there and say to the audience, "This is what I'm dealing with. It might not be the most flawless vocal you've heard in your life, but I want to be here." I'm welling up with tears talking about it because this is my life now. I don't feel like I explain that to the audience as an excuse, but rather a means to draw us closer. I don't want to curl up in a ball and disappear. The whole idea of perfection is overrated anyway. The audience wants to have an experience. They want to commune. Hitting a perfect high note isn't what moves people. My fans are affectionately called "The Debheads," and they've been with me through everything. I've got a pretty good life!

11

JAMES WILLIAMSON

(The Stooges)

By the time Williamson entered The Stooges in the late '70s, the band was already in the depths of drugs and destitution. As the guy who tried to hold it together, Williamson recounts the good, the bloody, and the time Iggy got his ass kicked by a biker.

Financially, we were pretty bad off and needed to get paid for gigs because we desperately needed to eat. There was this one Stooges gig around 1971. Our drummer, Scott Asheton, was driving the equipment truck for the first time. He just felt like doing it and didn't know anything about trucks. One of the first things you should learn is to check the bridge clearance when driving under one. The truck was a little higher than the bridge, and it didn't go so well. Luckily, no one was seriously hurt, but he smashed into the thing head-on and ended up in the hospital. He obviously couldn't make the gig that night, so we were without a drummer, but we did the show. Iggy started by asking the crowd, "Can anybody play drums?"

Steve Mackay, who played sax on the *Fun House* album, is the kind of guy who'll just say yes to anything. He said, "Yeah! I can play," but, of course, he couldn't. The songs we had aren't all that easy to play. They're pretty frenetic, and you have to know what's going on. We tried playing with Steve on drums, and it was absolutely horrible. Iggy spent the entire show trying to teach Steve how to play. We filled the hour, and while I feel bad about it, we still got paid. Our shows were always chaotic, so the crowd wasn't sure if this was just a typical night, only much worse.

We were not an act. Everything we did was for real and improvised spur-of-the-moment. We never had discussions before the show about how we needed to make that night extra crazy. We weren't an Alice Cooper-type band that had everything worked out. The roots of the band had more in common with a "happening." It was the late '60s, and things would just happen on the stage. After we developed a repertoire, it became a little more regimented in the sense that we had a setlist. Certain Iggy moves had been done in previous shows, but we never knew any more than the audience did.

I didn't personally witness the "peanut butter incident," but someone in the crowd handed him the peanut butter jar. I believe Iggy was on acid and smeared it all over himself. It's an incredibly iconic image, and it definitely wasn't staged. Everybody was doing psychedelics in the band, and I was no different. We tried it all. The first lineup of The Stooges, which was originally called The Psychedelic Stooges, were really into that, but they were mostly just jamming out and not playing songs. Once they made the first record and started playing the songs live, they were over that psychedelic period.

There wasn't much Iggy could do that would shock me. I'd seen most of everything, but one time we stayed at the Watergate Hotel in D.C. and played the venue right next to it. One of the girls that Iggy was dating gave him THC, and he was stoned out of his gourd right before the show. We were doing our best efforts to get him coherent for the show, but nothing was working. We got to the point where he could actually get on his feet, and we arrived at the venue very late. Backstage, the promoter was absolutely livid. He was so furious with us that he took off his Rolex and smashed it against the wall. He was screaming about how he'd see to it that we'd never play the East Coast again and all this craziness. Once again, we wouldn't be deterred, so we went on. Our road manager literally had to throw Iggy onto the stage. He was staggering around, and the first thing he did was fall off the front of the stage. Everybody in the audience thought it was part of the show, so they loved it. But, Iggy could barely even talk.

There's a lot of backstory to the time Iggy cut himself on stage. Mainly, his girlfriend was supposed to come to New York to meet him, then abruptly decided not to, which got him all upset. He didn't smash the glass; it was already shattered on the floor. He initially fell onto it, and when it didn't hurt that much—or he just didn't care—he started making all these little cuts on his chest. It was mostly just surface bleeding, but it definitely made for a gory scene. It creeped a lot of people out, and they were trying to get him to the hospital so he didn't bleed to death. I didn't feel that he was in any danger, but it's one of the things everybody remembers about the band.

Mostly, those kind of antics caused me a lot of frustration. That was a very low point in the band because some of us were trying to make a living doing this. My main focus was playing shows and making good records. We were trying to be professionals, and that kinda stuff was a little too out-of-control. That tour culminated in the show we did at the Michigan Palace. The night before, our manager had booked us into a small club near Detroit called the Rock & Roll Farm. None of us knew that it was actually a biker bar. Iggy was doing his thing out in the audience, and he slithered up to a biker who was leaning against a mirror.

We were accustomed to Iggy going into the audience and it taking a while for his vocals to come back. The biker had cold cocked him, and Iggy was out cold on the floor. The rest of us were on stage still playing the tunes, but after awhile, we began looking at each other, thinking, "OK...this is a little *too* long." Eventually, the crowd parted, and there he was on the floor. We didn't get paid that night, and luckily we got out alive. It was a really hostile night. Not to be deterred, Iggy went on the radio early the next morning and heckled the bikers.

All those bikers showed up at the Michigan Palace show the following night and immediately started chucking anything that wasn't nailed down at Iggy. Bottles, change, cameras...it didn't matter. That recording turned into the live record *Metallic K.O.*, which ended up being one of our most famous albums. That tour was really hand-to-mouth. We had our manager's credit card, which had long since been declined, but in those days, the instant communication wasn't there. We'd use that thing with no credit, run out on bills, and do whatever we had to do to keep going.

That lifestyle completely wore me out, and that last show at the Michigan Palace made us realize that we didn't need it anymore. It was insult to injury if you're not even getting paid to have beer bottles chucked at your head the whole show. That was the end of that phase of The Stooges. We had some demos that eventually got turned into the *Kill City* record in 1975, but that was really the end of it. I went on to work at Sony, where I got fat, dumb, and happy. In 2009, Ronnie Asheton died, and I had taken early retirement from Sony. It worked out to be the perfect time for me to come back and play with the band.

We did the *Ready to Die* album and toured together. It was fascinating because in the '70s, nobody thought we were worth a damn. When we came back in the 2000s, we were huge! The first show I did with the reunion band was in São Paulo, Brazil, for 40,000 people. I had never even been in front of 2,000 people in my whole life. My only thought was, "God, I hope I remember the chords!" I hadn't played guitar in forty years, so I had to do a lot of woodshedding before that one. A whole new generation had discovered the band, and there were a bunch of twenty-somethings at those shows, which was really cool to see. The next thing I knew, we were inducted into the Rock & Roll Hall of Fame.

We got all the accolades and vindication that we never got back in the day. It was really satisfying and strange. I'm always amazed at the influence we've had. People go ape over our stuff, and I feel weird because I don't know how to play guitar any other way. It's something I developed as a kid on my own, as a reaction to being a teenager. I don't feel there's really anything special about it, but others seem to think it's pretty cool. Who am I to complain?

12

JOHN BELL

(Widespread Panic)

One of the most venerable lifers on the jam-band circuit, Panic is the Southern roots alternative to the human peacock that became the Phish experience. Front man John Bell reflects on the scariest thing that can happen on stage: death.

It all comes back to Widespread Panic and my musical hero Colonel Bruce Hampton. The first time we played together was in 1987, when Panic was just starting out, at a little place called The Nick in Birmingham, AL. From the moment they began their set, some of it was noise, and some of it was music, and I walked to the stage like a zombie in *Night of the Living Dead*. It blew my mind. They were doing all kinds of weird stuff, like playing guitars with egg beaters, and Bruce was doing all kinds of crazy stuff while rocking out on this electric mandolin thing. It looked like a circus act, complete with on stage wrestling. Despite all the craziness, the music was cohesive. It blew my mind so much that I lost contact with how to play that night. I was totally discombobulated, to the point that it felt like I was trying to play during the last half of an acid trip.

It rocked me so much that the following morning, I seriously considered going ahead with Panic. I didn't think I could ever come close to what I had seen that night with Bruce. That night was a huge teaching moment because I learned to be comfortable with my abilities and not compare them to any outside entity. I don't know if it was ever Bruce's intention to teach, but I would always learn something in his presence.

Fast forward thirty years to May 2017, and Bruce celebrating his seventieth birthday with a concert at the Fox in Atlanta. It was the greatest collection of musicians I've ever played with, including Tedeschi Trucks Band, Warren Haynes, Jon Fishman, and Peter Buck to name a few. It was Bruce that brought all those people together because you never could have booked a night like that without Bruce. We had most of Panic up there on stage, and Bruce was the most on-his-game that I'd ever seen him. He was just playing on a whole other level. He was really present and killing it.

During the encore, Bruce had a heart attack on stage and passed away about an hour later. I wasn't at the hospital. I was driving there, just minutes away, when I heard he'd passed. That evening went from watching one of the best things happen to the worst. The weird thing was that it was during the very last song. It was one of Bruce's favorites, "Turn On Your Love Light," by the Grateful Dead. There were about thirty of us on stage for the encore, and my line of sight to Bruce was partially blocked when he hit the dirt. Some of the players around him thought he was pulling a Fred Sanford stunt, because he had done that in the past. There was a slow wave of recognition and understanding that something was seriously wrong. I was standing next to Susan Tedeschi who was singing. I just watched her slowly lower the mic from her lips and her jaw drop. It was a slow motion moment, but it happened really fast. We were all in shock, wide-eyed and teary at the same time. The night before, Bruce called me, and I realized it was a pocket dial. He said, "It was the weirdest damn thing! I just pocket dialed you and a whole bunch of people!" Then he proceeded to rattle off a bunch of names. He was always funny on the phone, calling me at random times on some weird whim or just to say hello. I've seen all kinds of great musicians—some that are humble and many that aren't. Bruce was the most genuine musician I've ever met. He was completely unafraid to be who he wanted to be and stand firm in his being.

The curtains closed, and there were 4,500 saying, "What the fuck?" It was my understanding that Bruce flatlined on stage but paramedics revived him. He died about an hour after that at the hospital. I had the opposite experience with our guitarist Michael Houser, who died at age forty from pancreatic cancer. The last shows were actually easier than I bet a lot of people think. I knew he'd been ill for a good, long time, so there was some time to process it. Even with chemo, there wasn't a great change in his physical appearance. That was another thing that distracted me from the reality of the situation. When we were playing, he was laser-focused and giving it everything he had, up until the last show. The shows really stand out for me as some of our best and not just because they might have been our last. He was soaring during those moments.

Originally, he had planned to not come out on that summer tour. We played Red Rocks and Wyoming, and he was stage four in those altitudes. Those altitudes are hard enough to deal with without cancer! After those gigs, he said, "I think it's time for me to go home." He never faltered during that tour. It's the little moments that I remember best and cherish the most.

13

JANE WIEDLIN

(the Go-Go's)

Much of the Go-Go's bad behavior has been well-documented, especially since they recorded much of it themselves via grainy, '80s camcorder footage. So, here's a story about disease, wheelchairs, and odd Japanese fetishes!

In 2004, the Go-Go's got invited to open for Green Day in Japan. They were playing stadiums and arenas, so it was super exciting. Japan is one of my favorite countries. Shopping is one of the Go-Go's main activities, so once we got there, we immediately went to an underground mall in Tokyo. It was completely sealed in, and we shopped our guts out. As we were walking back to the hotel, I suddenly started feeling like I was on acid. I asked the girls, "Do any of you feel like you're on acid? Did we get drugged?" Everyone, of course, said no. Back at the hotel, I was feeling weirder and weirder. I started vomiting uncontrollably about every thirty seconds. It was so bad that I didn't have time to breathe, and I thought

I was going to die because I couldn't catch my breath. The room was spinning around like a merry-go-round.

I was barely able to call Charlotte [Caffey], who is kind of like the mom in the band. She ran into my room, and we were just panicking. "What the fuck are we gonna do?" The tour manager arranged for me to go to a hospital, and when we got there, nobody spoke English. Not one fucking word. Here I was, trying to explain these symptoms to a doctor who doesn't speak English when I didn't even know what the hell was going on with me. They gave me something to try and combat the nausea, but I couldn't keep anything down. We had a show the next day, which was a theater show we were headlining without Green Day. I couldn't even walk, but the show must go on.

The Japanese have really crazy fetishes, and one of them is called broken doll. It's where really cute girls dress up with crazy, fake injuries, like broken arms and legs. I wanted to dress like a broken doll for the show. I put on this super cute, nurse's uniform. It was white with the red cross and the cute little cap. We wrapped all these bandages around my knees and elbows and put fake blood all over them. Because I couldn't walk, we had to get a wheelchair. I got rolled out on stage, wearing this insane outfit, and played the whole set like that. I was playing guitar, singing, while in a wheelchair in a bloody nurse's outfit, and completely nauseous.

One thing I'll say about playing while you're sick is that you're so locked in. You're concentrating so hard for that hour and a half, you forget that you're sick. I made it through the show, but backstage afterwards, I immediately started barfing again. When we got back to the States, I found out I had Meniere's Disease, which is named for the doctor who first diagnosed it. It's this thing where you have an acute, allergic reaction to something, but instead of getting hives or a stuffy nose, it goes straight into the inner ear. It causes massive vertigo and nausea. After getting it a few more times, we realized that when I'm in an enclosed space, like an underground mall or certain hotel rooms, there is a chemical used to freshen the air. I have a crazy allergy to those chemicals. When it hits, I feel completely lopsided. I can't even walk down the aisle of a grocery store. If I swivel my head, I fall over.

So, that's the craziest. There was one time back in 1979 when the poet Jim Carroll gave me cocaine before a gig. He was hot at the time, and he came to see us. He offered me the coke, which I had never done before. I think it was actually pure speed, because we were all grinding our teeth on stage so hard that we must have looked like total freaks. We played the songs three times faster than normal. That was the first, and last, time I took drugs before going on stage. It's never a good idea kids!

14

DARRYL MCDANIELS

(Run-D.M.C.)

As the first hip-hop group to go platinum, Run-D.M.C. went from playing
stadiums to barely filling clubs. To add insult to ego-bruise, McDaniels had
a crippling alcohol and Burger King addiction at the time and could barely
fit into his Adidas track suit.

This wasn't just the worst show of my life, but the worst period in
my creative and personal life. We called our 1990 album *Back from*
Hell, but I was still in hell. That record came out and nobody cared.
We were still getting booked because of the Run-D.M.C. name, so
we went on a little tour to promote it. We weren't playing the big
venues anymore. We were playing clubs, and some nights would
be five hundred seats. It was just a two-week run, and most of the
promoters were booking us because they were fans, not because
the demand was there. We rented a van, and with Jam Master
Jay's DJ setup trailing behind in a U-Haul, we were all crammed

in that thing. It was me, Run, Jay, our road manager, and a couple homies all packed in together, playing to basically empty clubs. We were Run-D.M.C. man. It was crazy!

From 1990 to 1993, we were playing to fucking empty clubs. Some nights we wouldn't even go on because the promoter couldn't pay us. Some nights we'd get the cash up front and play to twelve people. What happened was that instead of us just being us, we were trying to be something else. Hip-hop had changed, and with Jay being the flavor of the group, he started incorporating that New Jack Swing into it. R&B and hip-hop used to be separate. You'd have Keith Sweat and those guys in one corner, holding their own. New Jack melded all that together, and I couldn't stand it. It got to the point where every R&B record had to have a goddamn guest rapper. It's my opinion, but that shit is corny. Look at the damn cover of *Back from Hell*! Look at that shit! I've got on fucking checkered pants! We were not a tight unit: Run was a family man, I was running around drinking, and Jay was more concerned with his label JMJ records and trying to stay cool and hip. Jay was able to adapt to trends, but me and Run were clueless. Instead of just being Run-D.M.C., we were trying to conform to the trends, and it ruined us.

I look back at that time, and people will say, "D, it wasn't that bad." I say, "Motherfucker, it was worse!" We did a video for the song "Pause." The song wasn't that bad because it had that Run-D.M.C. energy. But in that video, Jay had me wearing a green and purple suit, doing the fucking running man dance. The last thing Run-D.M.C. should ever do is dance. It's fucking embarrassing! It was New Jack Swing, which had stolen hip-hop from us, and

I fucking hated it. Motherfuckers wasn't coming out to check us doing that shit! The Beastie Boys went back to instruments in 1992 with *Check Your Head*. They evolved, kept making Beastie records, and didn't let trends influence them. We forgot about our influences and totally bugged out.

We had a song called "The Ave." It was us trying to tap into gangsta rap. Again, it just wasn't us. We weren't the Geto Boys, and it was so phony. I knew shit was going wrong when Jay was telling me what to write about. They had me rhyming about crack and hustling. I don't do that! It sounded like a bad Chuck D or Ice Cube knockoff. I'm rapping about a 9mm and shit, when I want to rhyme about my new Gazelle shoes.

It was also the height of my alcoholism. During the day, I was drinking a case of forty-ounce Olde English. Not two or three either. I was so alcoholic I was buying that shit by the case. I put a refrigerator in the back of my monster truck so I wouldn't have to stop at the grocery store when I was drunk. Until I went to rehab and got sober in 2004, all of that drinking was just suppressing how I really felt. On top of my group falling apart, I was fucking depressed. I was drinking so much that I didn't even know I was depressed. When *Down with the King* dropped, I wanted to commit suicide! Life was good, the album was pumping, but I didn't want to do it no more. I was so fucked up that I couldn't even enjoy it. I was depressed since the '80s but didn't know it.

I was drunk and up to 240 pounds. Burger King became my favorite place in the world. I would order three triple cheeseburgers, a large fry, and large onion rings, because Burger King has the best onion rings. Then I'd get a fucking large orange soda and a large vanilla shake, which was all on top of the case of forties I was drinking. I would demolish it all in one sitting, and this was just during the day! At night, I was going out drinking rum and Cokes and fuzzy navels. You can drink that shit forever and not feel anything until later. I hate seeing pictures from that time, because I'm alcohol-bloated and huge.

Our saving grace came in 1993 with *Down with the King* and Pete Rock, who was killing at the time. With him as producer, we were back as the baddest motherfuckers around. The cool thing about Pete Rock was *Down with the King* did for Run-D.M.C. what "Walk This Way" did for Aerosmith. It put us back, man! We got back on MTV and the charts. We got back on the road and were opening for A Tribe Called Quest and Naughty by Nature, and back to kicking ass. I love Pete Rock. He saved my life. Funny story about Aerosmith. We were recording "Walk This Way" together. Rick Rubin wanted both of us there at the same time, not laying down separate tracks. When we first showed up to the studio and saw the band, me and Run said, "Oh shit, the Rolling Stones actually showed up!"

The whole thing came together so quick that we didn't know any better. I didn't know nothing about Aerosmith. Steven was very nice and said, "No, those are the other guys. We're Aerosmith." When the video came out on MTV, our fans were saying, "What the hell is Run-D.M.C. doing with the Rolling Stones?" I didn't even know their song was called, "Walk This Way." We'd just tell Jay, "Get out *Toys in the Attic* and play track four." We only knew that guitar riff. But those guys were cool in the studio and shooting the video. It was a culture clash, but we all were respectful and got along great. We didn't see any drug use, even though they've said that they fell off the wagon around that time.

When we got back on track, and back to doing what we do, Tupac and Biggie didn't want to close for us. We were opening, but they felt bad about headlining. The promoter said to us, "Help me out. Tupac doesn't want to close." Me, Run, and Jay had to go in the dressing room and tell Pac, "We're very flattered, but you hear that crowd out there? They're here for you. This is your time." Pac said, "The only reason I'm gonna close the show is because Run-D.M.C. told me to." We did a few shows with Biggie and he said, "Ain't no way I'm going on after you guys!" Big and Pac wanted their audience to see where hip-hop comes from. It was about respect, and that was very honorable of them.

The moral of my story is stick to what you do. Evolve and innovate, but stay true to who you are.

15

DEE SNIDER

(Twisted Sister)

This one I feel compelled to include a "trigger warning," as there is violence against women (not on Dee's part). The whole story reminds me of something out of the movie A Bronx Tale, *except Chazz Palminteri is played by Dee Snider in drag.*

In the early days of playing bars, our agent gave us the name "The Destruction Squad" because we would blow any band away that shared a stage with us. My first Twisted Sister outfit was Daisy Dukes, thigh-high stockings and leather boots, arm-length women's gloves, and a T-shirt that said, "I'm Dee. Blow Me." All that with very rudimentary, crude makeup, and a brown afro. Our thinking was that we would do, or use, anything to win. We were playing Amsterdam, Holland, with Anvil. The only time we were ever blown off the stage was by Anvil at the Paradiso in 1983. That, to me, was the worst gig ever. Respect to Anvil, but we lost in the ring that night. Holland was into much heavier stuff back then, and it was clear that the audience just wanted metal. They were really into heavy, black metal. We've always been a metal band, but with an anthemic, pop undertone. We went on after Anvil and just got shot down. Our opener beat us, and I'll never forget it.

Most bands are about sex, drugs, and rock 'n' roll. Our story is struggle, violence, and rock 'n' roll. Violence followed us everywhere. People's reaction to us was very visceral, and my reaction was the same. I was basically doing security while singing lead, because I would not allow any insult or slight at the band's expense. I was diving off the stage every night to get at someone. Most fights in bars are shoving matches, and most people who yell shit think they're protected by the fourth wall. Nope. From day one, I was ready to attack and, if necessary, I would physically address the situation. Back in the platform shoe days, I was about seven feet tall. For someone drunk and high in the crowd to suddenly be attacked by this loony in spiked heels and silver lamé was definitely a sobering moment.

The most violent night of my career was a post-show moment. Before we broke, we were a regional phenomenon in the tri-state area, playing for thousands of fans five nights a week. Being in a confrontational band, if you couldn't beat up the lead singer, or if the band embarrassed you in front of thousands, the response was usually to take revenge on their vehicles. Until we learned better, our cars were usually parked right by the stage door. The assumption was that it must be one of our cars, and they would smash windows, break antennas, windshield wipers, or slash tires. We started sharpening the metal on our windshield wiper blades to a razor's edge. I've seen people slice their fingers open trying to get at our wipers.

On this particular night, we had just finished our set at a club in Long Island. We had security and barricades at that point, and one of our security guys said, "We've got some kids here with a dead battery. They're looking for a jump." I went out to let them use my car and cables for the jump. I turned on the ignition and quickly realized that my car battery had been stolen. The road crew had the hood up of the kids' car, trying to get them going. I walked over to them, looked under the hood, and saw my car battery. It was a Delco Energizer with a cracked cap, just like mine. The odds of them having a cracked cap in the exact same spot was ludicrous. I said, "You fucking idiots. You stole my battery."

I have four brothers who often talk about stealing car batteries and siphoning gas—petty crime stuff, and we'd laugh about it. Now I'm thinking, "Is it still funny now that it's my car?" These kids didn't know—they were just looking for a battery. Before I could even come to a reaction on the situation, the crew went into action. They started beating the shit out of these guys. Since everyone, including our crew, had their cars scraped, kicked, robbed, and broken that night, it was them taking out all their frustrations on these people. I called them off, but at that point, their asses were kicked. But, this wasn't even the violent part.

We go back inside, and our drummer at the time—an asshole who will remain nameless—was beating the shit out of someone. He was kneeling on the ground, smashing the guy's face in. I had no idea who he was beating or what the situation was all about. The girlfriend of the guy getting pummeled is screaming and pleading for our drummer to leave him alone. Our piece-of-shit former drummer turns, looks at her, and straight-arms her right in the face, laying her out flat on the ground. I remember thinking, "Shit. Now we've got problems." You don't bad mouth someone's mother, and you never hit a woman. Ever.

Eventually, the girl started dragging her boyfriend away. I'm still trying to process all this. I go to exit the venue, and there are twenty-five people marching towards us. It's about 3:00 a.m., and they weren't there to be nice. They were carrying bats, boards, chains, and hammers, and they were coming for us. It turned out that our asshole drummer had mixed it up with some guys earlier in the pool room. This was a lynch mob out to get him. The girl had also told them that she had gotten punched, so it was gonna be war. These people, who were looking for a fight but not knowing exactly who they were after, now had an additional cause. Twenty-five guys approached us, and there were only about ten of us. An old school, street-fighting rumble was about to ensue. I rushed into the venue, yelling that we needed help. "There's a shitload of guys outside coming to get us!"

Behind me, I hear the door slam. It was the security guard of the club, which was run by these old mob guys. These crooked-nose, mobster, Guido-guys said, "Nobody's going outside." I screamed, "My band members and crew are out there! They're gonna get killed!" But they wouldn't let me out. All I could hear were the sounds of screaming, smashing, crashing, and glass breaking. When the dust settled, I was finally allowed outside. My band members and crew were laying on the ground, some badly hurt. The opening band, Zebra, had locked themselves in their car.

The mob had broken their windows out with bats and were hitting and stabbing them as they were trapped. Those guys all went to the hospital.

Our asshole drummer—the original target—was so banged up that he went to the hospital. There were broken limbs, blood, and teeth everywhere. It reminded me of the ending of an old movie called *The Wanderers*, after the Ducky Boys attack and leave behind a sea of bodies. This was not rock 'n' roll. One of the attackers had left behind their car, and the club was located on a canal. As a final fuck you, a bunch of us pushed this Monte Carlo off the dock and into the canal. It was righteous retribution. I had a straight razor held to my throat one night, but that night was the scariest.

16

ZAC CARPER

(FIDLAR)

When I first moved to LA in 2011, FIDLAR (Fuck It Dog, Life's a Risk)
were one of the most notorious, and rowdy, live acts. The party quickly
turned into a hazy, heroin death-trip, and lead singer Carper barely made
it out alive.

The weirdest thing that ever happened to me during a show
was on New Year's Eve. I can't remember which year, but we were
offered to play a show in Highland Park, which was five blocks
away from where we were all living in this recording studio warehouse. It was strange because this place was so close, but we had
no idea there was a venue around there. Since it was so close, we
started making this drink with Everclear and Tampico, which is
basically shitty fruit punch. We put it all in a fucking huge cooler
and brought it with us. It tastes like sweet rubbing alcohol. It's
horrible. We got to the place, and it was just a fucking trailer park

with no stage. We set up in front of the trailers and started taking this weird drug that was like fake molly. We started playing, and I immediately got an electric shock, because the whole thing was wired through extension cords. We could barely play because we were fucked up and getting moshed.

While we were trying to play, this older woman from the trailers came up behind us, pulled down her pants, and just shit right in front of everybody. To my right, there was this steaming pile of shit. She pulled up her pants and walked back to the trailers. We tried to play it off like, "Uh, that was totally planned. It's all part of the show." To top it off, we loaded up my fucking Volvo with gear, and it broke down. Then the tow truck driver was completely wasted, so I had to help him hitch the fucking car. It also sucked because I had just met this girl that I was into, and we were gonna go back to the warehouse to party. It was all over once the goddamn Volvo broke down. You don't hear about literal shit and bands much anymore. I think GG Allin took it to a whole other level, so people don't even try anymore. It's a shame.

Playing big stages or festivals like Lollapalooza is definitely not as much fun. It's fun to see that many people going crazy or the sound being great in a legendary venue. But I miss the days of playing the smaller, DIY shows because it's way more fun. It's like learning to play sober. I had to realize that if I was gonna keep doing this for a long time, I had to learn to not get fucking wasted every night. It sucks to say, but it's a lot more fun playing wasted. I've done it both ways, and it's just way more fun. Everything is way more fun. When I first got sober, I was really nervous about playing.

Every once in a while, I still throw up before shows, strictly because of anxiety. But right when we start playing, it goes away.

The thing about playing shows on heroin, and I think this is a universal, scientific truth, is that it kills your low end. You don't hear lower frequencies as well. It feels like you're floating, and it's a fucking horrible drug to play on. You can't hear shit. The best way I can put it is that it feels like you're being compressed. On top of that, you throw up a bunch. I was constantly ducking behind the amps to throw up during shows. Everyone knew what was going on, and I didn't try that hard to keep it a secret. I remember the day we found out China White heroin was in LA. We were doing a West Coast tour with Off! We only had black tar heroin in LA, so I was drooling. "Oh my God!" We found a bunch of white from Australia, and I bought a shitload of it. I was shooting up this China White dope every night before playing, and I only had a broken needle. The tip was fucking bent, so it was like I had to hook it into my veins. Super gross. I don't know about the air bubble thing with needles because I've shot a ton of air bubbles and didn't die.

Anyway, in the middle of the tour, I fucking ran out. I was kicking in the middle of the tour, and I was playing these shows totally dope sick. I remember Dimitri Coates, the guitarist for Off!, saying, "You're a dark motherfucker, man." That's all he kept saying to me. At one point, Keith Morris pulled me aside and said, "You're gonna kill yourself." Everybody knew, because I looked like I was kicking drugs. You can't hide that look. Did Keith saying that to me make any difference? Nope! We did a tour with the Pixies, which was about the biggest deal in the world to me. On the tour, I realized that I still wasn't happy. We played Lollapalooza, and I was still miserable. I went to rehab, and when I got out, I was all ready to just start shooting smack again. Right after I got out, I got a call from Billie Joe Armstrong of Green Day. He told me to stick with it. It was this weird happenstance of a random phone call that stopped me from tripping out about shit. Ever since that call in 2015, I haven't touched smack.

17

JARED SWILLEY

(Black Lips)

Black Lips could be viewed as garage-punk godfathers to FIDLAR, as they were the dirtbag kings of millennium male nudity, excess, and shock. Founding member Swilley recalls a gig SNL's Stefon would have loved: an illegal, warehouse space featuring Georgio, the Human Carpet.

Written by Jared Swilley

It's been about twenty years since Cole and I started playing shows as the Black Lips, and we had a long, slow climb to the middle, or whatever you wanna call it. Never quite made it to the top, but we made a life of it. In those twenty years it's kind of hard to pick the craziest show. There were more bad ones than I can remember, but this one sticks out. It was sometime near the end of 2011. We were all renting a place in New York City while recording our sixth album, *Arabia Mountain*, with Mark Ronson. It was our first time in a real studio and our first time working with

71

a producer, and that's a hell of a first producer to have. Still can't believe he agreed to do it.

We always say Black Lips can't have nice things, and there's some truth to that. One night after fucking killing it all day in the studio, we decided to go and celebrate at a Japanese joint that was near the studio. The last song we finished that day was called "Raw Meat," an ode to our collective penchant for raw flesh. Mark had never tried raw liver, so as a show of celebratory solidarity, he partook in the feast. That didn't go so well. The next day we all showed up to the studio, and the whole place reeked of death. We were all pretty sick, but Mark turned weird colors and couldn't really move. Turns out he was pushing 104 on the thermometer and had to go straight to the emergency room until further notice.

He got hauled off to Cedars Sinai. That left us in an expensive city, on the clock with nothing to do. Well, if a band is not recording, they gotta play, so we did just that. No legit club would book us with two days' notice, but we spent the better part of the first decade of our career playing basements, house parties, wherever and whoever would have us, so it wasn't something we were too worried about.

Now, the reason we weren't too worried about finding a place was due to the fact that when you spend a lot of time on the road, living like we did, you tend to run into some—and I mean this in the best possible way—shady characters that don't really go by the book, if you know what I mean. See, we had this old friend named Lonnie (name changed for the story). He was a career con man and criminal that spent a lot of time in and out of prison, with his longest stretch being around seven years. We loved and grew up with him. Good guy if he's on your side, but not someone you'd wanna go into business with or share your personal information. Still, a good guy in my book.

One of his sources of income was running an all-hours, illegal warehouse space in Brooklyn called The Shank. He had some tenants living there, a recording studio, drugs were sold, and they paid off-duty cops to tell their buddies to look the other way. I called up Lonnie and asked if we could do a last-minute show there with our friends Cerebral Ballzy, a hardcore band from east New York. He said sure, and it was on. What I didn't know was that he had been kicked out of the Shank about a week before, and the city had condemned it. Being the guy that Lonnie is, he made it happen. I shoulda gotten suspicious when we got there and he took out bolt cutters to open the door because he said he lost the keys. Classic Lonnie.

We get in, start setting stuff up, and there's no electricity. No problem. Lonnie gets two generators from the back of his truck, and we're cooking. We hook that up, I go to take a piss, and the commode isn't flushing. No plumbing in a warehouse that's about to have 800 beer-swilling bozos with busting bladders. I thought all was lost, but Lonnie knows some union guys down the road, and they get two porta-potties there within the hour. This was a very large warehouse, and the PA that we had was tiny. There was never gonna be a chance of hearing anything. Not that it mattered. We announced the show that day via whatever the popular social media platform was back then, and by 8:00 p.m. it was packed. There was a line around the block. Chaos ensued. It was supposed to be a five-dollar show, which was a steal for us at that time, but there wasn't really a door person.

Everyone kinda quit, and we weren't even supposed to be there. The only semi-legit thing was the off-duty cop, but even that was pretty sketchy. Inside, it was about three hundred over capacity. There was no place to move. No ventilation and no exits, except for a tiny front door beyond a narrow hallway. I started feeling lightheaded from all the spray paint. A team of graffiti guys came in with ladders and were spraying everywhere. Everyone was smoking, and it was a hot August night with no ventilation. I noticed that everyone—girls and boys—were using the back wall, or pretty much any available space, to piss. There was a river of urine saturating the entire floor. This was about 9:00 p.m.

It was around that time that I saw a rolled up carpet on the piss-soaked floor, and people kept running across it, laughing hysterically. Turns out, there was a man inside the carpet who was a well-known figure in Brooklyn at the time, and he got his kicks by going to parties and rolling himself up in a carpet and having people walk on him. That was "Georgio, The Human Carpet." It was finally time for Cerebral Ballzy to play, and that didn't last too long. It sounded like barely audible, static-fuzz farts, and the PA collapsed because of the mosh pit. Right after that, the shoddily constructed staircase collapsed under the weight of one hundred people.

We were up next. I had two friends post up next to my mic and PA because I knew our stage wouldn't last very long since it was two feet high, and it was dangerously overcrowded. The heat and fumes were almost unbearable. I'm not sure if we even played any cohesive songs. The mics had a life span of around three or four seconds, and it seemed like the crowd's goal was to destroy the stage and everyone on it. If I said we played fifteen minutes, that'd be generous. Maybe four or five songs, if you could ever call them songs. It was basically a huge, smelly fight where nobody had any idea who they were fighting or what they were doing. We were the centerpiece of the madness. It's a miracle that nobody got seriously hurt, at least as far as I know. I can honestly say that was our most dangerous and chaotic show. It was a total blast, but I wouldn't do it again.

I went to help clean the next day, and I can still smell it to this day. I do a lot of things to my body that can cause cancer, but I think being at The Shank that night was probably worse than a few decades of smoking.

18

NATHAN WILLIAMS

(Wavves)

Thinking about younger acts for this project, along with FIDLAR, Nathan Williams and Wavves was the first thing on my mind. In addition to a blackout Primavera set, Williams offers sobering advice to any young band, warning that mental and physical health is more important than a massive tour schedule.

Drunken, druggy, and rowdy is par for the course when it comes to Wavves shows. The most highly-publicized one was the first time we played the Primavera Sound Festival in Barcelona. Wavves started as a recording project in my parents' garage. I was twenty-one and making these records myself, without really thinking about a future, a band, or a career. I had no expectations. I was playing everything myself—guitar, bass, drums, and synths. I was producing everything myself, and the songs "No Hope Kids" and "So Bored," started making their rounds on the internet during the *Myspace* days in 2008. It caught on pretty quick, and I was suddenly signed and making money for the first time.

They flew me to New York, and I met a booking agent. They said, "Do you want to travel the world?" They had all these shows lined up. I said yes, even though I didn't have a band yet. I asked an old friend if he wanted to play drums, and we just went—nonstop. Nine months later, we're still on this first tour. I was completely running myself into the ground, partying every single night. There was a US run, then Europe, and I was getting drugs everywhere that I went. We finally got to Barcelona, and I found more drugs. I had a friend there that had a pill connect, and backstage they had Jäger on tap. At the beginning of the UK tour, I had gone to buy coke with a guy I knew in London. He went in with my money and came back out with a giant bag of Special K. I was like, "I don't want K! Why did you buy all this?" He said, "He didn't have coke, so this is what you get." There's no receipt or return policy when it comes to drugs, so now I had all this K.

Primavera was my biggest show at the time, and I don't remember playing it. I was on ecstasy, K, a shitload of alcohol, and whatever pills I was given. The last thing I sort of remember was being in a hot tub at a hotel called the Princess. The dealer for the festival was sitting next to me. He was the guy who would service all of the bands and their drug needs. He had pills, and that's the last moment I remember. There were probably 15,000 people watching me, which was probably their first look into what Wavves was, and I couldn't even talk. I couldn't sing and forgot everything. My drummer was pissed because I was fucking up and poured a beer on my head. I broke the mic and the mic stand. I think they just ended up cutting the set, shutting it off because it was such a mess. The audience threw shoes at me.

The next day, I cancelled the rest of the tour. I still had about four or five weeks left. That flight back home was insane. They thought about turning the plane around because I was sweating bullets and puking. I was coming down so hard. I went home and slept for about a month. When I woke up, *Pitchfork* and all of these publications that had been hyping me up, saying that I was a genius and a prodigy, were writing "Primavera Meltdown. Career over." It had only been a day, but they had turned a 180, gone polar opposite on me. A month later I released a song, and everybody was back on the train again.

There was another time in Germany. Our drummer at that time was antagonizing the crowd. It was a really small room, and we were all packed in. I think we had drunk too much during the day, and our drummer had gotten really pissed about a group of kids who were heckling us. He got completely naked, stood up from behind his kit, and started calling them Nazis. We had to get out of there pretty quickly after that. A couple nights later, I fell off the stage. The show was a complete mess. We went downstairs in the club and continued to party. In Europe, a lot of the backstage areas are downstairs in these cellars. I was playing monkey bars with the pipes and ripped one from the ceiling.

This awful sludge started pouring out, and we realized it was the sewer pipe. We filled the entire backstage with raw sewage. We might have been in Austria. None of us really knew where we were. The promoter ran in and started screaming at us in some foreign language. He was staring at this massive puddle of human feces, which was getting bigger. We grabbed our stuff and just peeled out of there. Needless to say, that guy never invited us back.

What really did me in was the touring. Nobody told me, "Hey, they're going to completely run you into the ground." I didn't know about setting boundaries with booking agents and labels. To them, all you are is a dollar sign.

19

TERRY ELLIS

(En Vogue)

I think we could all use a quick break from drugs and debauchery, so I present the tamest, and cutest, chapter in the book. I grew up with En Vogue as MTV/radio background score to my life, as I'm sure many of you, dear readers, did as well. Enjoy!

We weren't the wild and crazy girls, but I do have a good story. It was 1993, and we were on tour supporting Luther Vandross. One of the first things he said to us was that we weren't allowed to wear primary colors. That was the big one but also nothing too glittery or glitzy. We're like, "Uh...alright Luther." He never even gave an explanation for it. The only thing that we could come up with was that since we went on before him, it might seem like we were outshining him in the fashion department. But how could we do that? He was Luther Vandross! He was the headliner, and we were the opening act. It was our duty to follow the rules. He was very flashy and well-dressed on stage, which was kinda his thing. Luther and his backup singers looked absolutely stunning every night.

Before we hooked up with Luther, we had about two or three wardrobe changes during a show. When he laid down the rules, it changed the whole trajectory and flow of our live show. We were totally stumped as to what to wear. We had a show coming up in Houston, which was my hometown. Maxine [Jones] and I decided we were gonna break the rules because we were so drab on stage under the new orders. We all were wearing one boring, non-primary color or flashy outfit the entire set. Once we got to Houston, I said to Maxine, "You know what? We're in my hometown, and we gotta go out looking fabulous tonight!"

Me and Maxine hit the town, with only about two hours to go before we needed to be at the venue. We get to the Galleria, which was the huge shopping mall in Houston. At first, we were playing it safe, running around looking for halfway decent, non-primary clothes. We couldn't find anything because you can't really get around primary colors! We were shopping for the other two girls in the group as well, so we were literally sprinting from store to store. Max and I finally got to the Gautier store, but you're not gonna believe what happened.

We run right up to the glass doors of the store, but the doors are locked and the store looks closed. We start pounding on the doors like crazy people, and guess who hears the commotion and stares right at us? Luther Vandross and his people. He had closed the whole store down so he could shop. Max and I are standing outside the doors like deer in headlights, just peering in through the windows. We slowly started backing away because we were just gonna make a run for it.

They open the doors, and Max and I tried to play it off. "Oh, hi Luther! La-de-da, we're just out shopping!" We walked into the store, and it's Luther, his wardrobe guy, and another stylist. They knew *exactly* what we were up to, and they were getting the biggest kick out of it. Luther says, "Hi ladies! Just out shopping, huh?" We're like, "Oh yeah, we're just kinda looking around." Luther says, "What are you shopping for?" He's already nailed us, so we're like, "Oh, nothing special. Maybe just some shoes." Luther's wardrobe guy says, "Better not see you in any primary colors tonight!"

We found some amazing boots for Dawn in Gautier, which had to be inspected by Luther and his team. They ended up telling us that we couldn't get her the boots. We left and rushed to the venue. When it was showtime, we had to walk down a different hallway to get to the stage. We weren't allowed to pass Luther's dressing room door. As we're walking, Luther's wardrobe guy was waiting for us in the hallway. He was leaning against the wall, his legs were crossed, and he had one finger on his cheek. You can picture it, right?

He says, "Well ladies, you all look amazing. And look, there's the boots!" What he didn't know was that we had bought the boots for Dawn after we were told we couldn't. It's funny now, but I can assure you, it was torturous at the time. We weren't really offended, because we were so in awe of Luther and were huge fans. We just laughed it off and walked right on by the wardrobe guy. That was a big tour for us, and we were just really happy to have been invited. Like I said, we were boring. We went right back to the hotel after the show. We never went to any parties, and we don't drink. Not being able to buy boots was about the worst thing that happened to us!

20

MARK MOTHERSBAUGH

(DEVO)

As front man for DEVO, Mothersbaugh introduced flowerpot hats and jani-torial jumpsuits to the post-punk, New Wave scene of the late '70s and early '80s. Too arty for the punks and too weird for lasting mainstream success, Mothersbaugh has always been an oddball in a weird, beautiful world.

I've got a good drug story involving Andy Warhol. This goes back to 1977, prior to DEVO's first album recording. That whole summer we had been playing our first gigs at Max's Kansas City and CBGB, so things were starting to heat up for the band. This woman that was an A&R rep at Columbia called me and introduced herself. Her name was Susan Bloom, and I knew who that was because that summer in New York, after the gigs, I'd just watch TV. The only thing that was on late night in those days, before cable, was UHF, which was public access. Al Goldstein, the owner of *Screw* magazine, had a show called the Blue Channel. It was pretty wild and weird, with porn stars and underground New York celebrities.

The host of the show was Susan Bloom, who had this really sexy Brooklyn accent, big, beautiful curls, and large, pendulous breasts. I was in my early twenties and had only lived in Akron, Ohio, so she was the epitome of beauty and celebrity. She called up, and after inquiring if I had any plans that night, asked if I'd like to double date with her, along with Andy Warhol and Michael Jackson. I agreed to it, and she picked me up at my hotel room. She changed into this amazing dress and left her clothes, so I was thinking, "This is gonna be a great night." She immediately tried to find something for me to wear. After picking through my suitcase, she reluctantly decided the nicest thing I had was my janitor's uniform, which DEVO always wore on stage.

She took me to Studio 54, which was my first time, and I wasn't familiar with it at all. There was the big dance floor and another room where they served drinks. They had a little VIP section, which was like a sunken floor below a couple steps. It was roped off, and that's where we met Andy and Michael. Warhol had also brought this young man that looked like Li'l Abner. He was this shiny, buff kid wearing OshKosh B'Gosh overalls with no shirt. Andy was rubbing the kid's chest under the overalls, and the kid kept whispering to me, "Andy's gonna make me a star." Michael Jackson was very quiet the whole time. He was still black in those days and had a big Afro. He had just done *The Wiz* and was wearing a suede, Big Apple cap with patched, bellbottom pants, and enormous shoes. I wasn't into the outfit, but I loved his music.

I was wearing my stupid janitor outfit and looked like the custodian that had come to clean up vomit. I was feeling really self-conscious because everyone had these flashy disco outfits. All the music sounded like Donna Summer, and I couldn't differentiate one song from the next. Everyone in the VIP section was famous except me, and all these people keep rushing over to fawn all over Andy and Michael. They had all kinds of drugs, and cocaine vials were being passed around. The coke never made it down to me, but I wouldn't have known what to do with it anyway. I might have eaten it off the spoon.

A joint started going around, and Michael was sitting next to me. The joint came to him, and he just held it for a few seconds, staring at it quizzically. He handed it to me, and I'm from Ohio, where we didn't have any money. If someone had marijuana, it was a big deal. We'd go over to the house of the person with "killer weed," and there'd be a joint the size of a toothpick. We'd all drink a bunch of wine first, so when we'd get this tiny little joint, we'd be "enlightened." You'd take a hit, and someone would say, "Are you feeling it?" I'd be like, "I think so? Pass me some more wine." When the joint came to me in the VIP section, I hit it like I would have that tiny joint. I started coughing like crazy, and it was clear I was a total rube.

I tried passing it to Susan, but she was talking to someone really passionately, and I didn't want to interrupt. I took another massive hit and started coughing and drooling all over again. I tried to pass it to Michael, but he just waved me off. Susan suddenly wanted to dance. I said, "Oh, wait a minute. I don't know how." She tried telling me that I dance on stage, but I had to tell her that I was just making up all those moves in the moment. Gerry [Casele] and I did make our own choreography, but it was all rigid and stiff. It looked nothing like what everybody was doing on the dance floor. They all had these rubbery, liquid movements and looked great. It all looked very determined and professional, and it made me feel like an alien.

Susan grabbed my hand anyway and led me to the dance floor. I stood on the edge of the floor, and she went ahead and started doing all the disco moves with her friends. The lighting systems in those days were still really rudimentary. While this was one of the world's preeminent clubs, it still looked kind of ramshackle. They had this thing that was a cow jumping over a moon, a huge coke spoon, and all this crazy stuff. Above the disco floor, they had strobe lights and these big, colored light bulbs that looked like the signals at the start of a drag race. There were about a dozen of those rigs in the ceiling, and they were motorized so they could turn or lower toward the dance floor in a circle. They were rotating right over the heads of the dancers.

It was as cool as it got in the world of light shows back then. The light guy was really going at it, and making the lights do crazy stuff. He was spinning them really fast, and they were only attached by a thin wire to the ceiling. It started to look like a giant, multi-colored weed whacker was spinning just above everyone's heads, and I was starting to get very nervous. He brought them so low at one point, that I noticed people were getting whacked in the head. Blood was flying everywhere, and people were screaming. It was complete pandemonium. The song was playing way too loud, and I just stood there frozen on the edge of the dance floor. Susan was looking back at me smiling, just dancing like crazy. She was reaching out to me and wiggling her fingers, trying to coax me onto the floor.

She kept motioning for me to come out and dance, and I thought because she was in the middle of the floor, she couldn't see all these people getting clipped with the lights. People were slipping and sliding in all the blood, doing these crazy dance moves. I screamed out to her, "Get off the floor! It's a bloodbath!" She finally came over to me, asking what the hell I was screaming. I blurted out, "A bunch of people just got hit with those light fixtures and everyone's bleeding!" She seemed confused, and when I looked back out at the dance floor, everything was normal again. All the blood was gone, and there were no corpses on the floor. People were just dancing to some stupid disco song. She looked at me and said, "You didn't smoke any of that PCP, did you?" I said, "What's PCP?" She groaned, and hurried me back to the VIP section.

She said to Andy, "I think he smoked PCP. I better get him back to his hotel room." Andy just said, "Oh. How interesting." She got me in a cab and back to the hotel. She pushed me into my hotel room, screaming, "Good luck! I'll be back tomorrow for my clothes!" I just laid in the bed, completely rigid, frying. That was my first date with Michael Jackson and my *only* date with Andy Warhol and Susan Bloom.

21

PAUL OAKENFOLD

(DJ)

Arguably the progenitor of EDM music and culture, Oakenfold—with more than three hundred hikers—made the thirty-seven-mile hike through Nepal's remote villages and the Himalayan Mountains for a live concert, spinning a set at the base camp of Mount Everest.

Mt. Everest was definitely the craziest gig I've ever done. We had been working on it for a couple of years. It was really difficult to pull off because there were so many moving parts. We needed permission to do it. The time of year, with respect to the climbers, was crucial. Of the four charities I chose to do it for, two were local charities benefitting Nepalese children in the Himalayas because of the earthquake. The other two charities were London-based, representing youth and music. I didn't really want to talk about the project until proof of concept, because I've never hiked in my life. I've never slept in a tent. I'm a city boy. Preparing was hard for me. I trained for five months, hiking and working out. I had to learn breathing techniques because you're so high up. I asked how the equipment would hold up at that altitude, and nobody had any idea because it had never been done before. At night, it was sixteen below. It came together, and God willing, we pulled it off. I've only been back a few days, and I'm still exhausted. I'm physically and mentally drained.

I've never been a smoker. I drink, but I stopped drinking and got into a solid routine. I literally had never hiked before, so I had to knuckle down and focus. We raised a lot of money for the charities, and the Sherpas are incredible people. You talk about hard work. I had a backpack, but these guys were carrying equipment and everyone's bags, packs, tents, and food. They're born on these hills, and they're really nice, good people. It was a pleasure to work with them. After the earthquake, tourism severely dropped. Hopefully I proved that it's safe to go back up, and hopefully people will go on the trek of their lives. It really is an amazing adventure, and I'm so happy that I did it. If I can do it, I honestly think anyone can do it, if they have the will and determination. It will change your life in so many good, positive ways. Why shouldn't we all experience something like that?

I never thought that I'd be talking about that week, thirty years on, and the birth of electronic music as it's known today. We came back from Ibiza and started the whole thing. I was just a young kid inspired by the music I heard and inspired by the environment. I didn't want to leave it in one place. I wanted to continue to have those wonderful moments and feelings. That's really what it was all about. The generation of today is still doing it. They're still listening to the DJ, feeling the music and jumping up and down. It's the same thing as when we started it. The scene has grown up though. Electronic music has grown into a billion-dollar industry. We've done all the hard work, and we're here to stay. Look at the work of some of my colleagues who have big, commercial pop hits, like Calvin Harris, Diplo, Skrillex, and Avicii. They really know how to make great music, share it with people, and have become very successful.

However, I don't think art is corrupted by money. When I go into the studio, the canvas is blank. I want to come up with a creative piece of music. We make something from scratch. Let's say we make a great song and are excited about it. You want to share that song with the world. If the majority of people like it and it becomes commercial, then it becomes a hit. What's wrong with that? Do you want to go into the studio with me, and we're the only two people in the world to hear it? Do you not want to go back to your friends and family and say, "Check this out. Listen to what I did with Paul"? That's what music is all about! Music gives you a great feeling, and it's there to share. If you can put a smile on someone's face with a piece of music, then so be it. When I was on Mt. Everest and played music, there were people from all over the world in front of me. They were holding up their flags and coming up to me for photos. It was only about 300 people up there, but it was a special moment. I don't want to make music that I'm going to be the only fucking person listening to it. I want to share things with people and make them happy. That's what being an artist is all about.

22

PETER FRAMPTON

Scrambling to cash in on Frampton-mania, the young Englishman with the funny-sounding guitar voice thing was suddenly playing to over 100,000 rabid fans, resulting in a disaster straight out of the USO show in Apocalypse Now.

Right when we started to tour in the summer of 1976, which ended up being the big *Frampton Comes Alive* tour, there were some shows that had already been booked that weren't up to capacity because it was before the album really took off. I had played to huge audiences before in Humble Pie, but never as the headliner. Humble Pie supported Grand Funk Railroad at Shea Stadium, which was huge. We played before the Beatles. After I left the band, I started back at the bottom, so to speak. I was playing to 10,000–15,000 people, and almost overnight, it was 120,000 people in Philadelphia. That's a big audience, and so much preparation has to be involved. It was madness. For this one show in Austin, the outside area was only conceptualized to accommodate 10,000–15,000 people comfortably. It was a horribly built stage, and 80,000 people turned up. The mixing board was connected to a walkway off the side of the stage, so there were people climbing up on that. No one in charge had any idea what the hell they were doing. We had to be helicoptered in because there were so many people, as we couldn't drive in.

When we finally got on stage, the power was really bad because the grounding was horrible. Every time I touched the microphone, I got a bad shock. It was one of those "Oh shit" situations. All of a sudden, during the first encore, we heard this awful, cracking sound. It was people literally tearing apart the stage. They had pulled away the barricade with their bare hands because they were being crushed against the stage. Suddenly, there were all these people beneath us, and the stage started rocking, as if we were on some giant ship. It was about to collapse, and we were rushed off stage to the helicopter. Our girlfriends and wives were there waiting, but there was only room for us four guys and the pilot. The wives and girlfriends were not happy.

We squeezed in, and the pilot said, "Well, where are you going?" We screamed, "What do you mean where are we going? Isn't there some drop-off point? Get us the hell out of here!" The pilot responded calmly, "No. Sorry," and just took off. Obviously, we weren't from Austin, but we remembered that we took off from some kind of shopping center in town. At 1,500 feet, we were all trying to work out where the hell we were going as the stage was being destroyed below us. We were still in our stage clothes and were sopping wet. The pilot said, "How bout I drop you down here?" It was just the first supermarket parking lot he saw. We got out and said, "What do we do now?" We didn't have our road manager or security in contact, so we were just baffled.

The pilot just said, "I gotta go back and get more people." He took off, leaving us standing there with towels around our necks. Shoppers were staring at us like we'd just landed from the moon. We had to flag down a guy with a pickup truck. We climbed in the back and gave him the name of our hotel. He yelled, "Frampton! I don't believe it—I just saw you play!" Our wives and girlfriends eventually got back to the hotel, and believe me, they were pissed. Thankfully, no one was seriously injured. The area got five times the amount of people they were expecting, and it was just built on a local level. You don't get that with Live Nation now. It was my Altamont moment.

The most embarrassing thing that's happened to me on stage was in '77. We were playing Hartford, Connecticut, and that whole summer we had been playing outside during the day with a reflective stage. All our instruments were white, so there were no lighting rigs involved. After a short break, we switched to nighttime gigs. We were playing a racetrack in Hartford, and there were about 45,000 people in attendance. For our first nighttime show, we did what we always used to do. I would run onstage first, wave to the crowd, and pick up a guitar for three acoustic numbers. Then the band would come out. We did it the same way that night, and as I was not used to running on stage in the dark, the bright lights hit, nearly blinding me. There was no white line on the edge of the stage in front of the barricade.

I ran right on, and right off, the stage. I landed on the crash barrier as the crowd audibly gasped, "Ohhhhh." I finally got up and turned around, and my manager's brother ran on stage to pull me up. I put one foot on the front of the stage, and as he pulled me forward, my satin pants split from seam to seam. Because I wore them so tight in those days, there was nothing underneath. The crowd went from "Ohhhh," to "Ahhhhh," as I gave 45,000 people a proper mooning. I scrambled on stage and had to find some new pants. I was scraped from head to toe, but the show went on. That was my wardrobe malfunction moment...in a big way.

23

WAYNE KRAMER

(MC5)

The Motor City Five were one of the most outwardly political bands of their day, imploring a generation to kick out the jams, while inwardly destroying themselves with drugs and drink. Guitarist Wayne Kramer reflects on riotous youth, playing the 1968 Democratic Convention, and a nightmare tour with Johnny Thunders.

I really don't know where to begin. I have so many terrible experiences with bad gigs. Anyone who has played in a band, for any period of time, has stories like this. It's so hard to sustain a band and earn a living, let alone thrive and succeed. It's inevitable that you'll have so many bad experiences, and that's the reason so many people stop doing it, because it's awful. It's all great fun in the beginning, and even if you achieve some kind of recognition and make a few bucks, suddenly you're not the hot band anymore. I found myself discovering the painkilling properties of drugs and alcohol, and those contributed greatly to terrible gigs.

Towards the end of the MC5, I had lost my original inspiration. My idea was to be the greatest band in the history of rock and do something important. I wanted to have a positive influence on the world. Towards the end, it was easier to dull the pain. Going to the gigs really meant getting through the show so I could get fucked up afterwards. I had lost track of what I had set out to do. Band members left, but we had a final tour of Europe booked. I was in agreement with the guys that wanted to leave, but I wanted to continue to have a career as a musician.

Me and the other guitarist, Fred Smith, went to Europe to salvage what we could of the tour. We didn't even know the drummer. We met him in the dressing room of the first gig. We had a new bassist but no singer. Neither Fred nor I had ever tried to sing the MC5 songs. I had written many of them, but never sang them. Since the MC5 singer wasn't on the tour, we had to try and sing them. We didn't even know all the lyrics. Fred and I realized we couldn't do it, so we had to play standards, like Bo Diddley, Chuck Berry, or a simple, three-chord vamp.

There was no time to rehearse, and when we got to the venue, everyone was so happy to see us. We were the MC5 from Detroit... all the way from America! The dressing room had flowers and a full bar. The promoter was there with his family, and he wanted me to meet his kids. He wanted to have dinner after the show. Then we played and were just Godawful. It had nothing to do with the MC5. It was like some musicians who threw some shit together to play forty-five minutes to fulfill a contract. We went in the dressing room after the set, and the promoter was gone. The kids and the flowers were gone. The liquor was gone. Nobody was around to pay us because we were so bad. It was a nightmare, and my worst fears as a musician were realized.

I got into this because I wanted everyone to love me. Then everybody hated me, and I had to do it again the next night! In the MC5, it was really poly-substance abuse. It ran the gamut from hardcore alcoholism to crippling heroin abuse, and everything in-between. All drugs end up achieving the same end, which is to change the way you feel, because you don't like the way you feel.

Starting a band with Johnny Thunders was an impossible dream. I had just been released from prison, and I started a band with him. He wanted to call it Gang War, and it was like the mythical two leaders from two separate gangs joining forces. It looked good on paper, but the reality was that he was a practicing opiate abuser, and eventually I returned to opiate abuse with him. The band never had a chance, and it was another complete disaster.

It was ironic that we would play a small club somewhere in the Midwest, and Johnny would be brilliant. I would think, "This could work!" Then we'd play a really important show, and he'd be too fucked up to play. Our motto became, "Snatching defeat from the jaws of victory." But I have to say, there were many riots at MC5 shows. It was the '60s, and the youth were rebelling. The police were very violent, and any excuse to bust heads, they would do it. We played the Democratic Riot in Chicago in 1968. We played numerous riots in the Detroit area. A riot became a possibility any time there were 2,000 young people assembled, and the police would assert themselves. The shit would hit the fan. I never really feared for my life, but I never could tell. Let me add this: when you're smashing the States, keep a smile on your lips, and a song in your heart.

24

KING KHAN

(King Khan and the Shrines, The King Khan & BBQ Show, Louder Than Death, The Almighty Defenders, Tandoori Knights)

If you've never heard of King Khan, I implore you to read this chapter immediately. I guarantee, it will turn into your dark horse favorite. Khan chronicles his mental and drug-addled breakdown, which culminates in the flicking of Lou Reed's nose.

We were playing the Musicbox Lisboa Festival in 2016, which is this huge festival in Portugal. I was hitting the wine really hard that whole day, and remember I was drinking from the bottle with a straw. In the Shrines, we've got two Frenchmen and one who was born in Bordeaux. He was basically born in a puddle of wine, so when we hit the vino, it got crazy. This was a really mainstream festival, with Kanye West and all that. The day of our set, David Guetta was headlining, and he was DJ-ing atop this gigantic, neon pyramid.

Maybe it's because I'm bipolar or the fact that Guetta's music makes me aggressive, but at that moment, all I could think about was climbing that pyramid and tackling him. I was completely fixated, and I turned to Fred from the Shrines and said, "I'm gonna get kicked out of this festival. Tell my wife and kids that I love them." I got a running start and started climbing the pyramid. There were two big, buff security guards at the base of the thing, and they spotted me right away but couldn't intercept me. The pyramid was quite high, and I had scrambled up to the middle of it.

The guards finally caught up with me and threw me off the thing. I landed on my leg really badly, and I couldn't walk. I screamed and tried limping away. They started dragging me away, and the whole time I was trying to explain that I was an artist, but they just thought I was some crazy person. They threw me out of the festival. It reminded me of this one time that I pulled my pants down at some club in France. As they were throwing me out, I was screaming about how I knew Jean-Claude Van Damme. That security guard actually stopped and said, "Really?"

So, I get thrown out of the festival, but luckily we had a shuttle coming in twenty minutes to take us to the airport, so it was good timing. It was around three in the morning, and I was this staggering wine drunk with a busted leg. The shuttle van pulled up, and the whole band was inside. I hobbled in and started throwing up all over myself. We got to the airport, and my band guys helped me into the bathroom to wash off. I came out looking semi-normal but still couldn't walk.

I found an empty wheelchair right outside the bathroom, which was a miracle. I'm convinced God left me that wheelchair.

Fred was wheeling me around, and when we got to the gate, I told the attendants that I needed support getting into the plane. I was still viciously drunk, and there was a twisting ramp that led into the plane. Fred shoved me down the ramp, and I smashed into one of the corners, sending me toppling out of the wheelchair. Everyone boarding looked at me, and they were so shocked that this man had pushed a handicapped guy down the ramp.

The whole band was pointing and laughing, and none of the passengers or crew knew what the hell was happening, as there was also a language barrier. These people were horrified and thought it was some kind of weird hate crime. When we finally landed, I had to wait until everyone got off, and then this elevator thing lowered me off the plane. I kept thinking about the poor person whose wheelchair I had stolen. The rest of that tour I had to sing with a cane, and people thought it was some kind of pimp affectation I had adopted.

Here's a good Lou Reed story, and it begins with director Alejandro Jodorowsky. I was thirty-three, and this was in 2010, before I had been diagnosed as bipolar or properly medicated. I had become friends with Jodorowsky's son, and I was a huge fan of his dad. Not just his movies, but his philosophies and belief in tarot readings. I waited three years to accept his invitation because I didn't feel that I was prepared. Finally, one day I was ready. Alejandro had sent me this email about how to get to the house, and it was so intense. "Come to the door. Push the button. I will be there," it read.

I had slowly been losing my mind that year, but when you're going crazy, you don't really know it. I just knew something was wrong, and the non-stop touring and partying wasn't helping. Jodorowsky read my tarot cards, we talked for a few hours, he gave me a deck of the tarot de marsielles, and called me his "cher music-shaman". As I was leaving, he said, "You must be careful. This is the year of your crucifixion." That was it. I was like, "OK...thank you. Bye." It just felt so ominous, as those were his parting words, but believe you me, I was really mentally crucified about a month later.

At the end of the tour, we played the Primavera Festival in Barcelona and immediately had to fly straight to Australia for a festival that Lou Reed and Laurie Anderson had curated. We were one of the eight bands they chose, so it was a huge honor. The last night of Primavera, I had been partying all night with the Black Lips, and when I finally went to leave, there was chaos in the streets. It was a total Beatles moment as fans surrounded the cab and started banging on it. They're yelling, "King Khan! King Khan!" and the driver doesn't understand what's happening. We had about four hours to catch our flight, and I stepped outside the cab to try and explain that we had to leave.

The fans picked me up and put me on top of the car. I pulled my pants down, and because of my girth, I partially collapsed the roof. There were a bunch of cops around, and when I got back in, the cabbie was shouting at me in Spanish. I had two Spanish friends with me, who translated that the driver was complaining that I had broken his cab. As I'm trying to get the guy to pull over, he stopped at a police station. He had already called the cops on his phone, and ten cops walked out of the station and surrounded me. They took me in, and I had to wait for an English-speaking cop. He started reading me my rights, and I was freaking out.

I was trying to explain that I had to catch a flight to Australia to play for Lou Reed, but the cops didn't give a shit, or certainly didn't know who Lou Reed was. They put me in a holding cell, and I looked so ridiculous. I was wearing this weird, ill-fitting track suit and a necklace with fake shrimp on it. I looked like a complete freak. I was trying to explain to anyone who would listen that the whole thing was a huge mistake while begging for help to get out of there. An hour later, two Spanish cops approached my cell and started saying, "Foto! Foto!"

At this point, I'm just pissed but posed for the photo. One of the cops started playing "Blitzkrieg Bop" on his phone, and it was obvious they just thought I was some weirdo rocker. Suddenly, the guy says, "OK, you're free to go." As I'm walking out of the station, the cops are singing, "Hey, ho, let's go! Hey, ho, let's go!" One of them touched my shoulder and said, "Always remember the Barcelona police." Goes to show that the Barcelona police can be quite punk rock. The cabbie whose roof I bent insisted that he drive me to the hotel free of charge and played me all his favorite Johnny Thunders songs on his tape player in the cab, and we actually made our flight and went down unda!

When we got to Australia, I realized that I had some MDMA in my shirt the whole time and could easily have been arrested for it. At that point, I was beginning to realize that I really needed some mental help, but I just kept going. When we finally got to the Sydney Opera House to meet Lou Reed and Laurie Anderson, I was coming unglued. It was a couple days before the event, and they asked if I wanted to come hang out for some private rehearsals. I was still in shock that they were fans, let alone allowing me to watch a private rehearsal. I go in to this secret room in the Opera House and sat down next to Lou, who was singing. Aside from a piano player and a sound guy, it was only us, with Laurie on violin.

I hadn't slept in so long and had been partying, so I was basically crazy at this point. He sang a song I had never heard called, "The Vanishing Act," which, to this day, makes me weepy. When he finished this beautiful song, I turned to him and said, "Lou, that was amazing. But, you have something on your sweater." He looked down, and I flicked his nose with my finger. It's that thing you would do to a little kid—fake them out and flick their nose. I have *no* idea why I did it, and I flicked his nose kinda hard.

He's just starting at me, the way an ancient turtle would look when bitten by a mosquito. Finally, he said, "Please...don't ever do that again." I said, "Sure...yeah, no problem," and walked away from him. Then it hit me: What the fuck had I just done? I walked up to Laurie, who is super sweet, and asked, "Do you think Lou is pissed at me?" She laughed and said, "What, the nose thing? All the best uncles do that!" I sat back down next to Lou, and these four Tuvan throat singers by the name of Chirgilchin come in to perform for Lou and Laurie.

It was these crazy, super psychedelic, guttural sounds, and I was getting insanely sleepy. I kept pinching myself to stay awake, thinking how rude it would be if I fell asleep. I look over at Lou, and he's sound asleep, snoring really loudly. I took that as a cue, so I fucking nodded off. After we woke up, I got to do Tai Chi with Lou and his Tai Chi teacher Master Ren. The rest of the festival was pure insanity. I befriended a homeless, indigenous Australian guy on the street. I think he might have been on crystal meth, and

I brought him to the Opera House to meet Lou and Laurie, just another sign that I was losing my mind.

Lou and Jodorowsky are the two artists that have had the most influence on me and meeting them both in the same month just felt ordained. That year was a huge turning point, as three of my close friends had passed away. I was touring all the time, too, and hadn't grieved properly. It was all coming out during that Australia trip. I'd be talking to someone, and the next moment I'd burst into tears.

After the first King Khan & BBQ Show performance at the Opera House, I was wasted and brought all this Chinese food back to the venue. I dressed our tour manager up as a woman, in a wig and dress, and sent him out into the audience with all this food to serve people. We broke all the rules of the Opera House the first night because you can't bring food into the venue or bring people on stage. At one point, we invited all the Chinese women in the audience on stage. I had a rubber snake that I was throwing at the audience. I approached Lou and Laurie in the audience and brought them a tray of food after it had been poached by the audience already. Laurie was polite and ate some broccoli.

The second night was insane as well, and afterwards, me and BBQ broke up. The following morning, I had to go back and pick up some gear. Laurie saw me outside and sensed that I was in a weird place. I told her that the band had broken up and everything that was happening. Laurie told me to meet her back at the exact spot in three hours, as she had to go do a performance. I followed, and she did a whole concert for dogs, in this open space outside the Opera House. It was the most surreal thing I had ever seen. The dogs were in the first few rows, and she was talking to the dogs the whole show. She'd ask, "Which one of you dogs is afraid of thunder?" Then the dogs would start barking, and it was like they were carrying on a conversation.

It brought me back to a really beautiful place, and when I tried to go meet Laurie back at the Opera House, the security guards wouldn't let me in. They said, "You're that artist who brought all the food into the place and threw snakes. We have specific instructions not to let you back into the festival." I was about to cry again, and I yelled, "You can't kick Jimi Hendrix out of Woodstock!" (a line I had stolen from the late, great Jay Reatard). They didn't find it amusing and shut the doors on me.

I didn't know what to do with myself, so I was just pacing outside the Opera House. I started having this existential crisis, thinking, "What am I doing here? I'm a total wastoid." My tour manager called, and he yelled, "What the fuck are you still doing there?" I said, "I'm waiting for Laurie Anderson!" Apparently, they had been calling my tour manager all day, telling him that I wasn't allowed on the premises. They didn't want to call the cops, but they were giving him grief. Finally, Laurie's manger appeared and said, "Hey, King Khan! Come inside, Laurie's waiting for you."

When I finally got to her, I started bawling like a baby. She was very comforting, like a mother. I told her how I was banned from the festival, so Laurie and Lou became my babysitters for the rest of the festival. They'd say, "Who do you want to go see?" I'd sniffle and say, "The Blind Boys of Alabama," and off we'd go. If I wandered away from them, I'd immediately see the security guards get nervous and ready to swarm, so I literally had to stay with them as my guardians.

When I came home from Australia, I was unrecognizable to my family. I had a blond mohawk and black nail polish, rambling about how I was gonna quit music and join a Buddhist monastery. Shortly after, I was properly diagnosed as being bipolar and found the solace of medication. I've been relatively stable ever since, and I've noticed that the medication doesn't harm my creativity. That was the thing that I was most worried about. I thought that psychiatric meds would wipe out my personality. It hasn't at all, and I feel very lucky. I've had many friends enter mental hospitals and never return. I gotta thank my wife Lil and my two daughters Saba Lou and Amabelle whose support and love has made me an even better man than ever before.

25

DAVE KING

(Flogging Molly)

Kings of the drunken sing-along, Celtic punks Flogging Molly got their name from their early days playing beer-soaked dive Molly Malone's in LA. Front man Dave King has embarrassed himself plenty on stage, reflecting on a Spinal Tap-level calamity opening for Iron Maiden. No raccoons were harmed in the writing of this chapter.

This one still cracks me up. We were playing a show in Vancouver, at this beautiful venue right on the bay. We had this lighting technician at the time called Ned Sneed, who is an absolute fucking genius. He was having a nap on the couch backstage before the show, and from above him, out of the Styrofoam roofing, a raccoon dropped down right on his chest. Ned screamed and there was a brief scuffle before he was able to trap the raccoon in the bathroom. Bridget [Regan] walked into the dressing room, and there was this huge hole in the ceiling, and Ned was scratched up. She looked around and said, "What the fuck happened here?" We had to wait for animal control to come pick up the little guy.

We all thought it was hilarious, but I don't think Ned found it as funny. When we finally got on stage, during our second song, one of the guys from the first band was hanging off to the side of the stage, watching us. He accidentally tripped a switch which brought the front-of-house screen down. I think they used it to project football games or something on this massive screen, and it suddenly lowered down on us in the middle of the song. The guy who hit the switch didn't know how to fix it, so we were just hidden behind this screen. We stopped, laughed, and started playing "Folsom Prison Blues" until it got sorted out.

This next story is just one I thought was really cool. It was in Belgium, and we were doing this big festival with loads of stages. Just as we were about to go on stage, Black Sabbath was just finishing up. We were waiting in the wings, and someone from the band said, "Do we know 'Paranoid?'" We all agreed that yeah, we could probably figure it out. We walked out to 40,000 people, Bridget played the opening notes on her fiddle, and we launched into it. We fucking opened with it, and the crowd had no idea what was going on. It was brilliant. It was priceless. I used to know Ozzy pretty well, so I figured I could get away with it. It was just fun and games, and when we broke into our own songs, the crowd went mental.

The most embarrassing show was from when I was in my first band, Fastway, with "Fast" Eddie Clarke of Motorhead. I was a young kid, and we were on tour with Iron Maiden in Canada. We were already feeling the pressure, and a local radio station had asked if they could introduce us. We said sure, and one of their people came on stage dressed up as a huge bear, which was the station's mascot. One of the female DJs came out, leading the bear by the hand. This was back in the old days when you still used guitar cables, and the woman announced, "Ladies and gentlemen, all the way from the UK and Ireland...Fastway!"

Eddie Clarke started out the set, and he ran to the front of the stage just as the DJ and the bear were running off the stage. The bear couldn't see the guitar cable and tripped, falling flat on his bear face. There were absolute crickets in the audience. We thought the bear was dead, and our guitar tech was scrambling to get the fucking guitar plugged back in, so we could start the show. They had to drag the bear off the stage, and it was such a sorry spectacle. That was the how the show started, and it got worse.

At the time, Iron Maiden was using linoleum stage flooring, which covered the stage in a huge, checkered design. Somebody hadn't taped it down properly in one spot, and as I was running across the stage, I hit that spot. I was nineteen and not very graceful to begin with, and I tripped over that fucking linoleum and slid across the stage on my face. Suddenly, 20,000 people start laughing at me. They're all solemn and silent for the fucking bear, but not me.

I picked myself up off the floor and figured I had to do something really spectacular to win the crowd back. I had learned the microphone windmill from my hero Roger Daltrey, so I figured a big, microphone swing would look pretty cool. What I hadn't learned from Daltrey was that he tapes the microphone and cable together with gaffer tape, so it doesn't go flying out into the crowd. I started swinging it, and the fucking microphone flew right out at the audience. I'm just standing there holding the cable with no microphone, and we didn't have an immediate backup.

That was even more humiliating than my stage slide, and I was just dying inside. We limped off stage, and Eddie was fucking furious with me. He was just furious about the whole night, and he was cursing at me, "I'm gonna send you back on the fucking dole where I found ya!" We got on our bus, and he suddenly ran at me. There was a wooden cupholder on the bus, and as I ducked to get out of the way, Eddie whacked his fucking head on it. It knocked him out for about two minutes.

That was our dynamic, as I was a young kid, and he was an experienced musician from his days in Motorhead. Our drummer was Jerry Shirley from Humble Pie, who had tons of experience. I learned so much from them, and one time I made the mistake of putting the *Spinal Tap* movie on in the bus. I said, "I've got this great video—you guys have to watch it." They did not think the movie was funny at all. They turned it off, and couldn't look at it. I'm breaking my shit laughing, and they were cringing in pain. It was too real for them, and I don't think they understood that it was a mockumentary. What's great about that film is that it's true. Even to this day, I still get lost backstage occasionally!

Now we have a guy who comes and gets us when it's time to play, but in the early days, it was completely possible to get lost backstage in big venues. One time we were touring with AC/DC, and this happened during our first show with them. We were at a sushi restaurant the night before the show, and Fast Eddie got a little tipsy. He went to slam his hand on the table, and he accidentally smashed his hand right into a glass sake bowl. He was a bloody mess, and the next day he was in serious pain. The roadies had to gaffer tape the pick to his hand.

He thought he had ruined the tour, but you never heard a word of complaint out of Eddie that whole tour. He was such a great rock 'n' roll character, and I miss him dearly. We had a lot of good times, and it was a terrible shock when he passed. I didn't even know he was sick.

26

MIKE SHINODA

(Linkin Park)

Lead singer Chester Bennington's suicide in 2018 helped inspire a wake-up call about mental health in music that hopefully will inspire future generations to not forsake their health for art. In this chapter, bandmate Mike Shinoda celebrates the legacy of his friend.

One time on a day off in Japan, sometime in 2005, I was sightseeing with my wife and production manager, Jim. We went to this amazing temple, and I was trying to be incognito. I'm half-Caucasian and half-Japanese, and I didn't really feel like being recognized. We were just trying to have a chill afternoon. We came around the corner, and there was a group of about a hundred school kids. I'm ducking under my hood and trying to get around them without being seen, but the kids all ran up to us with cameras.

I'm thinking, "OK, we'll stop for a minute and do some pictures." The kids run up to me, hand me their cameras, and start posing with Jim. We didn't know what the hell was going on, but I shot pictures of a couple dozen girls hanging all over him. My wife was laughing hysterically, and as they were wrapping it up, I asked one of the girls, "Who is that guy that you're taking pictures with?" She exclaimed giddily, "Bruce Willis!" That was a nice ego-check.

There aren't a lot of big Linkin Park party stories. We never got super rowdy, but here's one of a handful, and once again, it involves Jim. It was the start of a tour early on in the band, sometime around 2003. We had a bunch of new crew members that had joined the team, and we were in Reading, Pennsylvania, getting ready to kick off the tour. We had done a soundcheck/dress rehearsal, and it was starting to snow really heavily.

The band was all back at the hotel, and Jim had rounded up the entire crew for a big speech. He told everyone, "Listen up. I know the kinds of tours you've all been on, but this isn't gonna be that kind of tour. These are family guys and very chill and clean. There will be no drugs or alcohol, and I don't want to see anyone drinking and smoking around the areas where the band might be. Please be respectful, and keep that stuff away from the band." Jim did his big speech, and I think he went so far as to say that if he caught anyone not adhering to the requests, they would be kicked off the tour.

As the weather got worse, we got snowed in and had to cancel the first tour date. The whole band and crew were stuck at the hotel, and I was chilling in my room. I got a call from our bass player Dave, who said, "Mike, you gotta get down to the bar right now." I asked why, and he said, "Just get down here now." I was kinda worried something was wrong, so I came down and the entire crew was in the bar. Dave, Chester [Bennington], and our videographer, Mark, are shit-faced.

I walked up to them and said, "Wow, you guys are going pretty hard. What are you drinking?" Dave yells, "Rainbow! We're on yellow, so you've gotta catch up." The bartender keeps serving up rounds of drinks for everybody, with these different colorful concoctions, and he's taking shots with the band and crew. Pretty quickly, the bartender was passed out on a bar stool, and Chester started tending bar. Jim looks like an idiot because the whole crew was now drunk with half the band after his big speech.

By the end of the night, we had thrown the keg out the window. We had started an epic snowball fight inside the hotel. A couple elevators were packed with a few rooms worth of furniture. I recall there was also a fire extinguisher fight. It ended with someone from the crew "acquiring" the hotel's security camera footage. I think there may have been animals in the bar by the end of the night too. It's not too crazy in terms of rock band debauchery, but it was wild for us, and one of maybe five wild nights in our career. It rarely happened, but when it did, it was really fun.

With Chester and I, it was really an opposites attract kind of thing. We were so different. He had such a rough childhood, and he ran with a really crazy crowd. I was a good student, and my mom was a court reporter. My dad worked as an Aerospace engineer who worked on space shuttles. As trite as it sounds, we first bonded over music, with our first loves being N.W.A. and Ministry. We obsessed over Depeche Mode, Nine Inch Nails, and Jane's Addiction.

Chester would walk into a room and radiate energy, and I always loved that about him. Anywhere we went, he would make things more exciting with his energy and volume. I was always slower to make a judgement call on something. I'll go to a movie, and it might be a day or two before I know my feelings on it. Chester was always zero to ten on everything. I could take him to any show or movie, and he would love it or hate it. There was no in-between. We'd make fun of each other for it, and I always loved that about him.

This is my first tour since Chester's death, promoting my first solo album. I did something that everyone on my team thought was nuts. I knew I wanted to add a multi-instrumentalist on stage, someone who could play all the instruments I play on the record. I also wanted a live drummer. I found the two guys that I wanted to bring on tour, with one being in London and the other in Israel. We couldn't get them visas in time to rehearse, and our first show was in Hong Kong.

Management was worried about what we would do, and we ended up rehearsing via videos and emails. For two weeks, I'd give them five pages of notes, and they'd send me iPhone videos, where they'd lean their phones against a wall, filming themselves playing. They'd send me that in a dropbox or text, and I'd send them back my notes. The day before the show, we finally all met in person in Hong Kong.

We had never seen each other in person, let alone played together. It could have been a fucking train wreck. We rehearsed for about four hours, and it totally rocked. It was a huge risk because after a few days, the wheels could have totally fallen off if we didn't like each other or couldn't vibe musically. The guys are awesome, the shows are incredible, and we're having a great time.

At every show, I've done a tribute to Chester by playing "In the End." Before the song, I talk for a little bit about him to set the tone, and I almost never talk about the same thing. For everyone, it's an introspective, deep moment, but I never want it to be sad. If a fan has feelings they want to get out, I want them to be able to cry, but I never want to feel like I'm bringing everyone down. Some people aren't there for that, but for me, it's very important.

Personally, I'm in a very good place. This tour has put me on a high. Having said that, it's a very delicate thing, and for months, I've walked the tightrope and performed that song each night. We were in Cologne, Germany, a couple nights ago, and I didn't have a curfew. We could have played as long as we wanted. It was one of the biggest venues on the tour, and we sold it out. The fans were hardcore Linkin Park fans, and I was playing random B-sides during the set, and they sang every word. They knew every single sound and syllable of every song.

We got to the moment in the set where I normally do, "In the End," and I felt like it was the right time and place to do something different. On the fly, I did a little medley where I played, "Heavy," "Numb," "Burn It Down," and, of course, "In the End." It felt like a religious experience. We were all sharing this very intimate and powerful moment that I can't express in words properly. There are no words for it. You can go online, watch the video, and get a sense of it, but it's something where you had to be there. That moment changed my whole outlook on how to play live.

It's not about playing songs off the record and just giving them a live version of the songs they know. It's a spontaneous, spiritual bonding that is bigger than the recorded music.

27

JENNIFER HERREMA

(Royal Trux)

The Sid and Nancy of the '90s underground, Herrema and bandmate/toxic boyfriend Neil Hagerty churned out scuzzy glitter rock, while doing enough drugs to shame Hunter S. Thompson. Heroin eventually tore them apart, but they reunited in early 2018 for their first record in eighteen years. Herrema reminisces about her time with the needle, and the damage done.

All of the weirdest, most embarrassing, fucked-up moments that happened to me on stage, I do not remember. I'm not kidding. All of the best ones, I don't remember at all. But, that's why they're the best ones. People have told me the best ones, and that's always when I was in another space. One that I do remember was in 1995, in Columbus, Ohio. Neil had a guitar tech at the time named Jim— an older man with a full head of white hair. He had toured with Neil Young and was a totally awesome dude. We were on stage, and he was trading guitars out for Neil. Suddenly, this chick in the front row got gnarly. She was yelling at our tech, "Get the fuck off the stage, old man!"

It was a knee-jerk reaction, and I didn't even think. I just dove off the stage and landed right on top of her. I started fucking whaling on her, and my jeans ripped, so my ass was hanging out. By the time the security came over, Jim had picked me up and put me back on stage. It was right when I was about to go into the second verse, and I hit it on cue. It was my most shocking moment because I shocked myself. I'm not a violent person, but I fucked her up. It wasn't a willful thing, where I was thinking about it for a few seconds. I never dive off the stage, and I had never beaten anyone up in my life. I got a reputation because of it, and it scared me because I wasn't in control of my actions. I played the rest of the show in cute underwear, with my ass hanging out.

I would black out a lot on stage. It was a combination of drinking, drugs, and heroin. It's like my subconscious has put those nights away forever. People would always ask, "Do you remember what you did the other night?" My response was always, "Uh, no." Neil would say things to me, like, "You laid down on stage and started tumbling like you were going down a hill." I guess I was rolling myself back-and-forth, but also singing, evidently. I have no memory of doing that, obviously. One time, when we were strung out in Ohio, I was standing at the front of the stage, and a wave of nausea hit me. Next thing I knew, I was projectile vomiting over everybody's heads. I was like, "Hello Ohio!" and then lost it. Poor Ohio.

We would shoot before going on stage, or basically, as soon as we could get our hands on it. In every city, we had someone to come to the show with drugs. I would forget what city we were in. On tour with Sonic Youth, I'd yell, "Hello Minneapolis" when we were in fucking Detroit. That happened a bunch of times, and that is the most embarrassing stuff for me, because it's just moronic. My pants split a bunch, and it wasn't just the time I kicked that girl's ass. I have no regrets, and it didn't bum me out at all to hear that I was rolling around on stage like a log.

On heroin, you just don't give a fuck. Your body feels so good, and you're just blissed-out. It feels like nothing could possibly go wrong. It was always just really relaxing to me. People say that you move slow and slur, but I didn't think that. It must have been the way it appeared. It's been such a long time since I've used or been on stage high on heroin. I drink and smoke weed now but not constantly. My husband and I grow weed. I drink socially, and my husband says, "You should probably do it at home." It's much more fun socially, and I can still go super next-level with it publicly, but that's not on the reg.

About seven years ago, with my other band, Black Bananas, we were headlining this festival in Portland. It was in this big-ass, beautiful old building, and we got in around 11:00 a.m. They had kegs and food, and we didn't have anything to do until our set, which was way later. I just started drinking and kept drinking. We found this arcade with a bar in it, but video games make me very stressed out, so I was just sitting at a table. It was a two-story arcade with black lights, and this guy walked up to me with two shots in his hand. He said, "I'm a big fan, will you do a shot with me?"

Like an idiot, I did it, and don't remember anything else after that. I do know that I was in the basement of the venue later on, and people were telling me, "You gotta play! You gotta play!" I guess I said, "OK," and the next thing I know was that people were freaking out. It was like I could see them in a dream, and the fire department and EMTs were there. I got roofied and was fucked up. I was out like a rock, and my body was dead weight. I could see stuff but could hardly move. That was embarrassing because there's never been a time when I couldn't play a show. That was the only time, and it wasn't cool.

It took a long time for me to get off heroin. It's not like you just say, "I don't like this anymore" and stop. The catalyst for me giving it up was that I had been shooting up in my hand for a while, and it got really infected. It got really swollen, and I got a fever. It kept swelling and turned red. I could see green pus starting to ooze out, so I finally went to a walk-in clinic. They needed to drain my entire hand, but I didn't have any money. I hadn't seen my parents or any of my family in years. There hadn't been any contact at all, but I called my mom from a fucking pay phone.

Basically, I told her what I'd been doing for the past six years and that I was calling from a pay phone in San Francisco. I cut off the communication because I didn't want them to know my life. It was my fault, but I wanted to shield them. I told her I was strung out on heroin, and it was such a relief when she said, "Oh! Is that all it is? We can handle this!" They thought that I had mental problems, which had caused me to walk away and stop communication. They were relieved that the only real problem was heroin. I flew home, and that was the first time I tried to get clean. They cut my hand open, and it was so gross.

They kept me in the psych ward for a week, and that sucked. Because my dad was an alcoholic, they wouldn't let me go home to my family's house when I was released. I was sent to Maryland, to a work camp, where female inmates go after they get paroled. That place was total bizarro-world. That was my first attempt, and I stayed clean for a while. I had to stay away from Neil, but of course, I didn't. I started using again, and the next thing I knew, I was on the streets again. I started living in a homeless shelter, but I had to leave because I had to piss test to stay there.

At that point, I did a cold turkey at my friend's house, and she basically locked me in a room. I had to get away from Neil again, but it was a cycle. I'd stay clean for a minute, get back with Neil, and start over again. Neil and I had bought a farm in Virginia, and I went off the rails again when my dad died. I was supposed to be in a movie, so I flew to Los Angeles and didn't leave. I had insurance through the Screen Actors Guild, so I went to some fucking Malibu rehab place with it. I ended up going to four rehabs, but the last time, I checked in sober. I wasn't on any drugs, but one morning I woke up with my best friend dead on top of me, and I just lost it.

They put me on antidepressants, and I had never taken them before. That's really when things changed, and it was the end of the heroin cycle. I had been self-medicating all my life, and I understand that now. I was always aware that I was different, and even as a kid I knew it. My sister would wake up with the sun shining in the morning, bouncing around, but I never wanted to get out of bed. I never wanted to take a shower. It was just impossible for me to care about anything. Music was the one thing that really gave me energy. Once I opened up and expanded my brain beyond the melancholy, punk-rock teen mindset that I had placed myself in, music took me out of my depression. It saved my life, for better or worse.

28

BIG DADDY KANE

With Mack Daddy swagger and dextrous flow, Big Daddy Kane made the ladies swoon and the guys jealous. His ladies-man persona inspired an ill-fated 1991 Playgirl *spread, resulting in homophobic backlash that basically killed his career. But he's still doing his thing, and Kane reflects on hip-hop's golden age and a very scary female fan.*

The craziest thing that ever happened to me with a female fan was in Detroit in the late eighties. She was just staring at me the whole show and made her way backstage. It was like she wasn't even blinking, with this crazy, serious look. We started talking, and I invited her back to the hotel. We're in the room, and I told her that I was gonna take a shower real quick. When I was done, I opened the shower door, and she was just standing right in front of the door. It was steamy in there, so I didn't see her and hadn't heard her come in. She had that same crazy look. Then she said, without blinking, "I just want to wash your back."

I'm standing there, dripping wet, and said, "Excuse me?" She said it again, "I just want to wash your back. That's all I want to do." I said, "You know I just took a shower, right?" She didn't say anything and stared back. I said, "I'm actually good." She took this long pause and said, "It doesn't matter. I just want to wash your back." Now, I'm scared. I put on a towel and started looking around the bathroom to make sure I hadn't left any hair in my comb and checked my pockets to make sure she hadn't taken anything for some voodoo shit. She said it again, "Can you please let me wash your back?" I said, "Can you just hold on one minute, please?" I went to my security dude's room and said, "Yo, come get this crazy-ass girl out the room, please!"

In my mind, I wanted to be a super-lyrical, serious rapper starting out. I wanted to amaze people, like the way I would do on street corners in regular rap battles. I thought that would come across well on the stage. When you're battling on the corner, the people in that small circle can hear every word you're saying. On the stage, it's coming through loudspeakers with 500 people in the room. I started out doing club and house parties with Biz Markie, as neither one of us had a record deal at the time. Biz wanted me to do funny rhymes on stage. He wanted funny stuff about girls, and I had those, but it wasn't the type of rap that I wanted to be recognized for, as that was his thing. One time, we were opening up for Doug E. Fresh and Slick Rick, and I refused to do the funny rhymes. Slick Rick had just put out "La Di Da Di" which was funny rhymes about girls.

Once Biz started beat-boxing, I went into the super-lyrical, fast-flow, Big Daddy Kane stuff. I was just spitting, and that's when I realized that Biz knew what the hell he was talking about. I watched people in the crowd turning and walking away. We were an inch away from getting booed and, from that day on, I learned that all that serious stuff is cool, but there's gonna be people in the crowd who can't get every word. You need to stick to what's simple, what works, and can captivate the crowd in that moment. I learned a lot that night about being a performer, and it stayed with me. I learned the hard way.

Me and Biz were doing shows for a production company called Mike and Dave, and we were doing shows around Long Island, the Bronx, and Harlem. We were taking the train to get to the shows, and we didn't have any money. We were always hopping the turn-stiles, or we would walk from car to car, hoping the conductor wouldn't catch us because we couldn't afford tickets to where we needed to go. Sometimes there'd be a stage, sometimes we'd be on the floor. One time, we performed on top of lunch tables. Rob Base was there, as he didn't have a record deal either. We came home with stripper money that night—only one-dollar bills—because it was only kids at the show. They were paying us fifty dollars to perform with their lunch money. Imagine two dudes on the back of the A or F train with big knots of dollar bills in their pocket. It looked like a fat wad, but it was pretty embarrassing.

That was the crack era, in 1984. There were definitely drug dealers in the crowd, but it was a party. People weren't just smok-ing crack on the floor. It was cool, and even the cats that were hustling came to party. I'd see them on the floor doing the wop, the running man, and even the cabbage patch. People left their beefs outside unless they didn't like the record playing. There would be thugs, gangsters, drug dealers dancing their asses off, enjoying themselves. But if you played "Brooklyn's in The House," by Cut

Master D.C., or "Top Billin" by Audio Two, I don't know why, but it just triggered something in cat's minds. They'd hear that beat, and it was suddenly like, "I gotta rob everyone." I'm serious—these were the two chain-snatching songs. Those songs came on, and dudes would lose their damn minds. They would snatch your gold chains, your girlfriend's earrings, and it made those dudes in the crowd violent.

If it was an entourage of people, they would wild out, snatch somebody's stuff, and pass it off to one of their crew. He'd pass it to someone else, and that person would stash it until they were ready to leave, in case security was searching people. If it was only one or two people, they'd punch you in the face, snatch your shit, and run straight for the door. There wasn't jealousy on the scene, but we were all competitive. We'd be doing a show with LL Cool J, and we got to rock hard. L would have explosions and fire lighting up on stage, and we didn't have all that production. We had to take it to the next level energy-wise.

We all used to rock a club called Latin Quarters, and the wildest night I remember is when they tried to rob Jam Master Jay. It had to have been about at least ten of these cats going at Jay and the Beastie Boys' guy, DJ Hurricane. Jay had the gigantic, big rope chain with the Adidas on it, and they were trying to get it. Jay was just there hanging out, and I swear, he looked just like Jim Brown when Jim was on the Cleveland Browns. Remember how you'd see Jim running, and there'd be six people on his back? That's how Jay looked, fighting off all these people that were jumping on him from different angles. I saw glasses smashing, chairs flying, and the music stopped. All this commotion was going on, and they cleared the whole floor out.

I gotta give props to Jay because at the end of all this, when the smoke cleared, he still had his shit on his neck. Jay was stocky but short. But, they didn't get him. He fought off ten Brooklyn cats that night, going hard on him. They never got him, and you gotta respect that.

29

IAN ANDERSON

(Jethro Tull)

Ian Anderson has an incredibly dry, deadpan wit and had me laughing out loud during the interview. This is one of the funniest chapters, in my humble opinion, but prepare for urine and flying tampons.

In 1975, Jethro Tull was the first band to perform at Shea Stadium since the Beatles had a really tough gig and decided it was over. They couldn't hear themselves over all the screaming and shouting, and they were going through the motions. They felt bad about it, is what we were told, and they put an end to that kind of touring. A few years later, we appeared at Shea Stadium and suffered a number of problems. The audience was very far away because they weren't allowed on the field, only in the stands.

In one way, I felt very close to a certain member of the audience that day. As I was waiting in the alleyway to the dressing room, about to walk out onto the field and run over to the stage, I was suddenly drenched in liquid. Someone had tipped something over from high above, and it got all over me. At first, I could only assume it was beer, but I quickly learned it was urine when the smell hit me. At that moment, I got my cue to run to the stage, stinking of someone else's wee-wee. I'm sure that the person meant well, as it was a generous offering of bodily fluids to speed me on my way.

That was a pretty uncomfortable show because it's not very nice to smell bad, nor is it very pleasant to play wet, as it was all over my hands, my guitar, and my flute. Somebody out there knows that they did that to me. I'd like to meet that person today, just to discuss the matter, as gentlemen do. Another embarrassing situation, this time that the audience was well aware of, was at an arena show, but I can't remember where. I was performing on stage, and suddenly I felt something hit me in the chest.

I was wearing an open-necked shirt, which was open down to the middle of my chest. Something hit me, but it wasn't very hard, and it didn't hurt, so I carried on playing. After a bit, I looked down and saw blood. My first thought was, "My God—I've been shot." I thought the adrenaline had kicked in, and I wasn't feeling the pain. I thought that I was probably going to die very soon, so I figured I'd carry on playing as long as I could. These poor people had paid good money to see a show, and I better not cut it short just because I'd been fatally wounded.

I went on playing, and the first opportunity I had, when I wasn't playing anything, I pulled my shirt open and looked down. The first thing I noticed was something that looked like a little piece of string. I pulled it, and out came a bloody tampon. I had been hit by a freshly-plucked tampon. I held it up so the audience could see it and threw it over my shoulder. I kept going, but as the show went on, I was thinking how extraordinary the whole thing was, as this blood was wet, so it wasn't like someone brought an old tampon to throw.

This was spur-of-the-moment, and the mental process that someone went through to do that really impressed me. I was also blown away by the incredible accuracy of the throw, as it hit me square in the chest. It could have deflected off my pants or something. Like the urine, I had to think of it as an act of enduring love and adulation. A woman was sharing her most intimate, personal elements with me on stage. I suppose that if I was being cynical, I could look at it as something quite nasty. They didn't really like me, and that was the ultimate insult. Come to think of it, I'm not quite sure how I feel about it now. I'm not aware of the tampon culture in North America.

Those two things did happen back in the seventies and haven't happened since. I'm actually curious how many artists have had experiences with flying tampons or pint glasses of piss dumped on their heads. I know that guys like Tom Jones and Englebert Humperdinck used to get underwear thrown at them, but I've never personally gotten any undergarments thrown at me. It's not a Jethro Tull thing. I suppose our audiences have usually been a bit more well-behaved. I've heard of girls lifting up their T-shirts to expose their breasts to performing musicians, but that's never happened in my experience. The best I get is maybe a flicker of a smile from the ladies, but that's about it.

Drugs and alcohol were never part of my story, but it's part of my story growing up. When I was at art college before I became a musician, the guy sitting next to me in class had heroin needle marks on his arm. I had to ask what it was, as I thought he'd been bitten by some strange creature. It always filled me with fear that addicted people were caught up in something that didn't make them better painters or artists. When you read about the history of art or music, particularly jazz or blues, there are constant references to drugs.

It plays a major part in artist's lives and a very major part in their downfall. Many people that I've performed alongside came to a sticky end. I remember we were on a show with Graham Bond in 1968, and when the sax player took a solo, Graham shot up on stage. He didn't even shuffle off to the side to do it. He stayed at his keyboard and just turned his back a little bit to the audience. He wrapped a leather strap around his arm and shot up. To a young lad like me, that was deeply shocking. I saw him twice more in his life, with the last occasion being just a couple weeks before he threw himself under a tube train in the middle of London. That was a very sticky end...because it was messy.

A year later, in 1969, we did a few shows with Jimi Hendrix. When I first met him, he was a very polite, quiet, calm guy. The next year, after we did the Isle of Wight Festival, he was found dead of an overdose just a few weeks later. In such a relatively short time, he went from some presumably controlled habits to a straight downhill run. Those are the object lessons in life that these people taught me.

You've got to have a lot of luck on your side to dabble with serious drugs and get through it. There are those that get through it, and people who make the mistake of thinking, "I can be like

Pete Townshend and do serious drugs. Then, I'll just stop and be cured." They think they can be Steven Tyler or Elton John. It was never difficult for me to say, "No, thank you," when someone offered me a joint or some pills. If someone presses a glass of single malt whiskey in my hand, I'm probably going to drink it. That's about it for me.

There's a fairly good chance I'll spend my last days on a morphine drip, so I'll experience what Class A drugs are all about when that happens. I'll let you know if it was worth the wait.

TUNDE ADEBIMPE

(TV on the Radio)

It's hard to think about the early 2000s without TV on the Radio on the soundtrack. Actor and performer Tunde Adebimpe takes us back to that heady time, when cocaine and free love were the main course in post-9/11 NYC.

I'm gonna go chronologically with my embarrassing stories. We'd been signed to Touch and Go Records around the end of 2002. Usually, the way that Touch and Go did things was to see a band live and make the decision whether or not to sign them. Corey Rusk had already heard what we were doing because Dave Sitek was roadie-ing for the Yeah Yeah Yeahs. 9/11 had happened, and no one was going outside. During that time, we made an EP that sounded like an actual record. He played that for Corey, who loved it. He signed us right away, and we were the first band that he'd signed without having seen us live.

There's a big difference between sitting in a bedroom studio and putting things together piece-by-piece versus having an actual live band. We didn't have the live band because I was singing and using a loop pedal. Dave had a sampler, and our first shows were at this club called The Stinger in Brooklyn. Those early shows were essentially just a free-for-all. We had a monthly residency there, and all the shows were basically a big fucking mess.

We would take song suggestions, and the shows would sometimes end with complete strangers onstage holding microphones, totally drunk, while trying in vain to play our instruments. We'd be sitting in the booth watching them, saying to whoever cared, "That's TV on the Radio." It was more like poorly rehearsed karaoke. We'd leave the drum machine on, and it'd be a bunch of drunk, coked-up white kids trying to rap over it. We were not a polished live act.

Kyp Malone joined the band right as we were getting signed, and we decided to go out and play the whole EP a cappella. We hadn't rehearsed enough for any of it to sound good, so our live show was an even bigger fucking mess than before. It was three guys behind briefcases with microphones, and it was horrible.

We took it to Chicago, and our first show playing for the label, we were opening for The Fall at the Empty Bottle. Corey was really excited and kept saying how much he loved our EP and how talented we were. Five minutes into the set, and it was already a complete mess. Ten minutes in, it was even worse. People were touting us as the next big thing, and you could see the wave of disappointment as it washed over the crowd's faces as we kept playing. One of the keyboard stands went down, fell into the audience, and we were scrambling to set it back up. It was ugly. You could tell everyone was wondering how we could have had such hype behind us. Afterwards, we went up to Corey and sheepishly said, "Yeah, that was kinda rough." The look on his face was a mixture of terror and confusion, and you could almost hear him thinking, *What have I done?*

Corey had to admit that he'd give us another shot. If that wasn't embarrassing enough, we had to walk past Mark E. Smith from the Fall, who basically told us we sucked. If that guy says you're a mess, you're a big fucking mess. There's a strange sense of calm that comes when you're onstage and realize that you're totally failing. You just have to keep your head down and finish. The worst thing you can do in that situation is stop. If you finish, there's at least the hope that people might think that what they just witnessed was exactly what you intended. People might think it was some weird, stylistic choice to go up there and completely suck.

Quite magically, sometime around 2003, it was like somebody landed with forty barrels of cocaine and began distributing it all over Brooklyn. I was suddenly being offered this shitty eighties drug every night. It wasn't my thing, but everyone was doing it and suddenly becoming talkative assholes. One night we were playing at this place called Star Foods on the Lower East Side, and the place had that coke vibe, where everyone was going crazy.

I remember seeing two people sitting on one of our monitor amps on stage. It was really crowded in there, so I figured they had climbed up for a better vantage point. At first, it looked like they were making out, but I quickly realized they were having sex on our amp as we were playing. I got away from that side of the stage pretty quickly. It's not like you tap someone on the shoulder and ask what they're doing in that situation. The crowd realized what was going on, and we all just kind of watched the couple go at it. It was kind of like a freak show, where you know you shouldn't be watching it, but you can't look away.

There was no S&M-type vibe to that place either. It was more like an eatery, but that's just what was going on at the time. There was a lot of public sex going on post 9/11. The vibe was that if we were gonna die, we might as well be getting laid in the streets. One time after a show, I remember standing on a street corner and hearing this chain-link fence rattling behind me. I turned around, and it was two people who had just left the show going for it against the fence. That was Brooklyn in 2003.

On our second tour of Europe, we were playing a festival in Rotterdam, so, of course, we had to stop in Amsterdam first. It was still so mind-blowing that you could legally purchase weed, and we really went for it. We got some really powerful stuff and got high before going onstage at Rotterdam. This was the last time I ever got high before a show because I was so stoned that, after playing only three songs, I thought we were done. I thought the show was over. I just walked off the stage and left everyone behind. No one had a clue what I was doing or where I was going.

I left the stage and walked right out of the venue. I strolled down some avenue and went and sat down in a park. I sat there and watched these kids run around the playground. I was thinking, *Man, that was a crazy show.* I hung out in that park like a weirdo for the better part of an hour. Eventually, I walked back to the festival. Everybody was yelling, "Where were you? What the hell happened?" I was so confused and sputtered, "Well...we were done, so I left."

They said, "Uh, no. We weren't done, and we were all standing onstage, wondering what happened to you." They thought that maybe I had gotten hurt, and they were all looking for me backstage. Our manager was completely freaked out and was off searching for me. We went to Sweden after that, and someone came up to me and said, "We heard the rumor that you smoked too much powerful marijuana in Rotterdam and walked off the stage!" I really wish there was somehow video of me in that park, having this introspective moment—this weird, sweaty man, watching the kids play.

31

AL JOURGENSEN

(Ministry)

After my interview with Al for the book, I immediately googled "Al Jour-gensen + Overdose + Lollapalooza 1992." Nothing came up about the overdose, so I contacted his publicist, who was blown away. We had never heard the story, and Al had never shared it publicly. Prepare for the craziest of the crazy, folks. It's a doozy.

Let's start out in 1981, which was the last hedonistic days of the castle that was Studio 54. It was probably one of the last shows that the Studio hosted, and it was one of Ministry's first. How we got that gig, I have no idea, but I do remember this: we were completely freaked out to be playing this really famous place. The show was on a Tuesday night, and there were only four of us in the band at that point, so we had backup tapes with us to help fortify the sound. Backup tapes back then weren't on computers, but on a four-track tape machine, and those tapes were our bass sequencers and other sounds.

At that point, this show was going to be the most important gig we'd ever done, even though it was in the complete decline of Studio 54. They were gonna be shut down within the year, but to us Chicago guys, having only four or five gigs under our belt, it was a huge deal. We knew about Warhol, Grace Jones, and all the famous people that hung out there, so we were completely freaking out. We were working with a new monitor guy that night, who was recommended to us, but he was really cocky. He kept saying, "I know how to run the tape machines!" He totally looked down on us, and it was obvious he thought he was slumming it with us rookies. He was a real asshole.

Before the show, Andy Warhol came backstage, so we got to meet him. He was on coke or some weird inhalant, but he was cool and exactly how I imagined he'd be. We get on stage, and there were only four tracks on our tape machine. One was a click track that was specifically for the drummer. The other was a bass synth, and one of the others was some sparkly sound effect. The new, cocky, asshole monitor guy put the fucking tape on backwards. The click track was now blaring at 120 decibels to the crowd. All that anyone could hear for our first song was basically a really obnoxious-sounding cowbell, played in reverse.

I realized it right away, and I kept yelling and motioning at the guy to cut it. The guy flipped me off! The pit in my stomach was the size of the Grand Canyon. My first time at Studio 54, and Ministry's first time in New York City, and I bolt across the stage and dove like fucking Superman into the monitor pit. I literally started strangling the fucking monitor guy. The great thing about New York and Studio 54 at the time was the audience thought the whole thing was some kind of weird performance art. I had one hand on the guy's neck, and I finally shut the tape off with my other hand. Then, we fought for another minute or two.

I finally popped back up, and I grabbed a guitar tech who actually knew how to run the tape machine. He switched the reels, played it forwards, and we soldiered on, none the worse for wear. But man, what a fucking let-down. It was the most embarrassment I had ever felt in my life, but I don't think the audience cared. I think they honestly thought that every Ministry show started with me beating the shit out of the monitor man.

That fear has never gone away. Forty years later, I'm scared shitless before every show. These people have paid good money to see us, and I want to represent why they bought that ticket in the best possible way. Starting out, I had no idea what to expect every night. That suspense made an already anxious person like me, anxious on steroids. I really fucking hated those early years playing live, and I'd probably live to one hundred if it wasn't for those early days. The stress alone probably took twenty-five years off. That's why I gravitated to downers and psychedelics, just to get out of my own head. The other part was after being on the road for three months. What do you do with the other nine? Keep self-medicating! It certainly helped, because anxiety is debilitating. To have people judging you while you're baring your soul on stage is fucked up. So, I was medicating a lot, which brings me to my next story.

In 1992, Ministry got added to the Lollapalooza tour. I was a full-blown fucking junkie. I was doing at least eight-to-ten shots a day, with a $400 a day habit. We were scheduled to play right before the Red Hot Chili Peppers. I was in the dressing room doing my pre-gig heroin shot. This particular batch of heroin I had scored in St. Louis, or somewhere off-the-radar, and I wasn't expecting a huge level of potency. It's like today with that fentanyl crap. I'm telling ya, this stuff was *heavy*, and I went down like a rock. I shot it ten minutes before the show, and usually, it would just calm my nerves. This stuff deadened me, and I was barely breathing. I wasn't dead, but whoever ran the tour back then didn't want the hassle of calling the paramedics or dealing with the publicity. To try and get me onstage, my tour manager had to buy some crack. He had never done crack before, but he was inhaling it and blowing it into my mouth to wake me back up.

Those festivals run like clockwork, so if you're not onstage, you're fucked. If you miss your set, your career is fucked. It's not necessarily true, but they make you think that. So, my tour manager is working on me, blowing crack into my mouth, while I'm lying prone on the dressing room floor. The Red Hot Chili Peppers roadie, I forget his name but God bless him, had long dreads like me. He took the cowboy hat off me, went onstage, and sang the first three songs of Ministry's set as me. Nobody in the crowd knew the difference. He saw me on the side of the stage after the third song, after they had resuscitated me and quickly gave me back my cowboy hat. If anyone was paying close attention, they would have seen that suddenly I was wearing completely different clothes. The show kept going, and it turned out to be a really good one! That guy saved the show—and probably our career—by pulling it off.

I don't think Perry Ferrell had any clue what was going on because two days earlier, I had thrown him out of my dressing room. We got there around 5:00 p.m., and we were set to go on at 8:00. Perry was in our dressing room alone, wearing only a bath towel, shooting heroin. We had a very heated exchange, and I haven't seen Perry since that day, when we almost came to blows. I was a junkie too, so I understood, but pick somebody else's dressing room!

I want to end on a positive story. It was the last show of our first Australian tour, in Perth, sometime around 1995, on the Big Day Out Festival. As we went onstage, it was right as the sun formed a half-moon on the horizon of the ocean. It was an outdoor venue that looked right out at the ocean, and this gigantic sailboat was cruising past this burnt-orange sun. The crowd, about 30,000 people, had lit this massive bonfire in the middle of the mosh pit and were dancing around it like *Lord of the Flies*. I remember looking over at the band and saying, "It doesn't get any better than this." There are so few goose bump, spine-tingling moments like that. It had all come together, and it all made sense.

The next morning, we had to fly to Japan. I had decided I didn't want to go, so I handcuffed myself to a railing in the Perth Hilton. I had thrown the handcuff keys out the window into the shrubbery. My poor tour manager had to dig around in the bushes to find it and get me out of there. That moment on stage in Perth was so perfect that I didn't want to leave. I was set to live there for the rest of my life. The road crew tackled me, opened up the handcuffs, and pushed me into the plane. Our plane landed on the day, on the minute, on the second of the Kobe Earthquake of 1995. The plane started veering all over the place as we touched down, shaking violently. We had to stay in that airport for twenty-four hours, as the venue had been destroyed. I knew something bad was going to happen because the most beautiful thing had happened the night before in Perth.

32

ROBIN WILSON

(Gin Blossoms)

I'm thirty-seven years old, and I've never heard someone say they hate Gin Blossoms or "Hey Jealousy." If you're reading this and you do, please hit me up on social media. I'd be very interested to hear what turned your heart so cold.

I've heard that it takes ten thousand hours to become an expert at something, whether it's quantum physics, guitar, or skateboarding. It's like college and grad school combined, and I'd say that I've definitely logged over ten thousand hours learning songs, so that might be my big skill. When you start out in a band, you're so far from being an expert, but the excitement is so strong that you just don't care.

In the spring of 1993, we were on a particularly brutal tour, where we were playing college campuses in the daytime and clubs at night. This went on for about three months, and it was completely exhausting. We were all stuck in a van together for at least twelve hours a day. One guy would get sick, and it would work its way around the van over the course of a couple of weeks. We'd get sick and then well again, but by that point, somebody in the front of the bus had a whole new sickness, which would start the whole cycle over again.

We were literally always sick on that tour. It was a very exhausting and depressing time because it felt futile. It was only a few months before "Hey Jealousy" took off, but it didn't feel like we were accomplishing much. In the end, that tour did have a lot to do with the band breaking, but at the time, it just felt like we were spinning our wheels. There was a show somewhere in Florida, and I hadn't really spoken to anyone in the band for a couple of weeks. I was just sick, depressed, and tired.

We were all drinking heavily on that tour, and there was plenty of pot going around, which was how we were spreading the illnesses in the van. Those were our only real vices. No one was doing any hard drugs with any regularity. We're playing in Tampa, and I was just pouting my way through the show. I wasn't having any fun, and in between songs, I had nothing to say to the crowd. I was so pissed off and depressed that I was ignoring them.

We were about to launch into "Hey Jealousy," and there were a few moments of dead air. I was standing there fuming. Our bassist, Bill Leen, looked at me, knowing I was losing it. He gave me a shrug that implied, "What's the deal?" Off-mic, I said to Bill, "What am I supposed to say to these people? That I don't give a fuck anymore?" Bill stared at me incredulously and yelled back, "Fuck you,

Robin!" Right then, we launched into "Hey Jealousy." That happy riff started right as we were cursing each other out.

I look back at that as one of our lowest moments. Now I can look back on it in amusement, but at the time, I was breaking down. I just didn't want to be there. The band formed in late 1987, and I joined in March of '88. I was hired on a Wednesday, and we played the next three nights straight. For the first show, I only knew eight songs. Originally, I joined as the rhythm guitarist, but after a few months, I became lead singer. I was so relieved because I was so far out of my league as a guitar player. That night in Tampa, it felt like we had been plugging away forever with no results.

We signed to A&M in 1990 and released an EP in '91. We recorded *New Miserable Experience* in the early months of 1992. It was released in October of '92, and we were in the van from October through the next year. It was a very slow build, so when the record finally broke, we felt like we had earned it. It wasn't an overnight success by any stretch, which made the success sweeter. In the '80s, there were alternative bands like R.E.M., The Smiths, and the Pixies. In the '90s, the people who had been working at college radio stations now had commercial radio jobs.

That's when the programming flipped. Cheesy metal was dominating commercial radio, and suddenly alternative became the new form of popular music. I think it was due to those college music geeks getting real jobs. Nirvana was obviously the watershed moment. In the winter of 1991, we were on tour supporting our first EP, *Up and Crumbling*. We were playing places like Wyoming and Montana and driving all night long.

We had to put snow chains on the van tires, but we didn't have the right size. The ones we put on made this incredible noise, and the inside of the van was like being inside a drum. It was so damn loud. I was sitting in the middle of the van. I turned around, and our guitarist Doug Hopkins and drummer Phillip Rhodes had taken pillows and wrapped them around their heads, securing them with belts as a sort of headband. That was their remedy for dealing with the noise.

We were somewhere in the Dakotas at night, and I had finally fallen asleep. Our tour manager was driving, and Hopkins was shotgun. The moment I woke up, I heard Doug say, "Well, here we go." Right at that moment, we slid sideways off the road on a patch of ice. We crashed into a ditch next to the freeway. It was so perfect how Doug had casually narrated us sliding off the road. Later that same tour, we had bought a bunch of fireworks on our way through New Mexico. Each van had a bunch of bottle rockets and Roman candles, and we were firing them at each other as we drove.

Both vans were driving side-by-side, and the goal was to get the bottle rockets and candles into the windows of the other. We pulled over on the side of the road to pee, and it was the most beautiful night. We were hundreds of miles from the nearest city, so the stars were bright. It was the most stars I've ever seen in my life. We were standing in the snow, shooting off all these bottle rockets. I had wrapped myself up in my blanket, and I just stood there, watching the fireworks. I had my Sony Walkman, and I was listening to Nirvana's *Nevermind*.

It was the second time that I had really listened to the album, and I remember that as one of the magic moments in my life. The stars shining down, with the light shimmering off the snow. We were young and laughing, shooting off bottle rockets. I can still remember that sensation of complete satisfaction. There was nowhere else in the world I wanted to be at that moment.

Doug's alcoholism started affecting our live shows soon after. One time, he was in the middle of a solo and threw up into his own mouth. He inhaled it and got really sick. He was in the hospital for weeks with pneumonia. There were times when he would just abandon the show. Doug didn't care much about his equipment, so his cables and effects pedals were really fucked up. They were constantly shorting out, and he didn't replace or repair anything.

For as much pride as he took in the band, along with his guitar playing and songwriting, there were so many things that he was lazy about. Early on, we were playing this frat party. It was a speakeasy theme, so all of the kids were dressed up like the cast of *The Untouchables*. The fraternity was on probation, so there was no alcohol. It was the most sober show we had played at that point, and we were feeling kinda stupid. There were only about twenty or thirty kids there, dressed up in silly costumes.

We were on stage, and Doug's equipment was so bad that if I stepped anywhere near his effects pedal, it would short out. He started getting mad at me, saying that I was screwing up his equipment. He yelled, "Don't do that!" I yelled back, "What? All I did was move!" He told me to stay the fuck away from him, and at some point, I was feeling good and jumped in the air as I was singing. I landed with a thud on the stage, and Doug's equipment shorted out.

He started screaming at me again, calling me a motherfucker and everything else. There was no way I was going to allow him to blame me for this, so I got right in his face. The show came to a grinding halt, and I jabbed my finger into his sternum really hard. I screamed, "This is *your* fucking fault!" That physical show of aggression on my part caused him to completely lose his shit. He yells, "I'm gonna kick your fucking ass," but he stormed off the stage instead. We thought he left, and these college kids in their stupid gangster costumes were staring at us, completely shocked that we had derailed on stage.

We figured the show was over, so I went outside to have a cigarette. Doug was sitting alone on the staircase fuming. After twenty minutes of arguing, we limped back on stage and made some attempt to finish the show. There's a lot about Doug's death that's really private, and a lot of it is still really painful for me. What we're now realizing is that Doug was bipolar. We didn't know that at the time. We had no way to predict how he was going to behave, and he became very jealous and bitter towards me in particular.

This was a notorious moment in the band. Few people know about it. Doug and I had written a song together called, "Hold Me Down." To this day, it's one of my favorite songs on *New Miserable Experience,* and it's the only song that Doug and I share co-writing credit. We wrote it as our first single and wanted it to sound like Cheap Trick and The Replacements. Doug went off and wrote the verse and chorus, then turned it over to me. I wrote the second verse and threw in the bridge, which is a direct Cheap Trick ripoff.

When we finally got into the studio to record the album, Doug was out of it. His alcoholism and depression were runaway, and he wanted to rewrite all of my "Hold Me Down," lyrics. He didn't want to give me the co-writing credit, but he was too lazy and fucked up to do it. My version of the lyrics got recorded, and we were in the control room arguing. He said to me, "If I even liked you, I would give you half of 'Hold Me Down'." That was so hurtful to me, and the whole band was shocked. Everybody looked like they had been hit in the face.

We knew that something was terribly, terribly wrong. We thought we were never going to be able to finish the record. Doug wasn't even in the band when the record came out. His alcoholism was so out of control that we had sent him home. He was still fighting for sole credit on "Hold Me Down," and he called me up one day. He said, "You get to go on tour. You get to be in the band. All I have is the publishing, and I want full credit."

I said, "Doug, this is something we did together. I won't take any of the publishing money, but I am taking my credit for that song." He screamed at me, "You coattail-riding son of a bitch!" Then he hung up.

Privately, he would confide in other people that he knew he had brought everything on himself. He spent his last days talking shit about the band and that I had ripped him off. Where he had so much talent and was, in many ways, the leader of the band, he didn't have it in him to move to the next level. He could have stepped up and been one of the biggest rock stars of our generation, but at some point, all of his problems got away from him.

We did manage to reconcile before he died. The band was talking about releasing "Found Out About You" as the second single, which would have been August of '93. I came into town and really wanted to talk to Doug about it. I didn't want it to be the single if Doug didn't support us doing it. I asked a friend to connect me with

Doug, and within twenty minutes, Doug showed up at my house. There was a lot of tension, but we got to say our piece. I know that I said my piece to him. We only saw each other twice more before he died.

I'm proud that I still get to sing Doug's songs and that they're a part of people's lives. As a grown man who's been through a lot, I look back and wish we could have worked it out. I wish I could go back in time. I regret that I didn't have more time with Doug as a songwriting partner, and I can only imagine what we could have done together. Mostly I look back on those days and smile. I think about the fun stuff, like that time out in the snow, shooting bottle rockets at each other. That night was magic.

33

JOEL GION

(The Brian Jonestown Massacre)

For those unacquainted with the West Coast psychedelic-folk scene in the '90s, director Ondi Timoner's 2004 documentary Dig! *was the perfect entrée into the dysfunctional world of The Brian Jonestown Massacre. Here, the band's tambourine-wielding troublemaker, Joel Gion, fondly recalls the time that he almost broke up Oasis with his "super speed."*

Back in the early days, I was constantly on speed. In 1994, two years before filming started on the *Dig!* documentary, I was working at Reckless Records on Haight Street. Oasis's *Definitely Maybe* record had just come out, and I was really into it. I saw Oasis was coming to San Francisco, so I phoned our manager and said, "You've got to get us on this bill!" This was before "Wonderwall," and they hadn't had a huge hit yet. It was this cool underground thing at the time. They were playing this small 200-capacity club called Bottom of the Hill. We all knew the club owner, so she got us on the bill. *Definitely Maybe* was released two weeks before the gig, and suddenly, that venue was way too small. It was their first time in America, and people were going bat shit.

Like I said, I was on speed all the time, and I had been up for three days before the gig. I was super excited to meet them because I kept reading about how they were really into drugs, especially coke. I thought, "If they're into that shitty English coke, I'll blow their minds with this crazy crystal meth I've got!" We pulled up to the venue for soundcheck, and their huge bus was parked outside. I knocked, and Noel Gallagher opened the bus door. I said, "Hey man, I'm in the opening band, and I have the most righteous speed you'll ever do!" I was all stoked to walk right in, but he said, "No, we only do coke." I stood there stunned, and he shut the door in my face.

Our guitar player at the time, Jeff Davies, was a heroin lifer. He'd been doing it since his early twenties. While I was trying to meet Oasis, he went off to score. He missed soundcheck, and it was getting pretty late. Meanwhile, a female friend I used to do speed with all the time had met Liam Gallagher outside. She had gotten on Oasis's bus and had given them a bunch of lines of this crazy speed. Jeff still hadn't gotten back from scoring, and the show was oversold and completely packed. Coincidentally, Pulp and Blur were on tour together and had played a show across town the night before. Both bands showed up for the show. Damon Albarn was going out with Justine Frischmann from Elastica, so it was this whole scene. It suddenly had turned into Brit-pop central for one night.

With no Jeff in sight, we had to go on. We're playing without our guitarist, and suddenly Anton [Newcombe, lead singer] yells out, "Jeff! I see you motherfucker! If you're not up here in ten seconds you're out of the band!" Anton had been watching the door the whole time, waiting for Jeff. He started counting down on the mic, "Ten, nine, eight...." The crowd joined in on the countdown, like it was some kind of fucking rocket launch. Jeff is this little guy, and he had this huge rockabilly bouffant at the time. I could see his hair trying to get to the stage in this insanely packed house. He was climbing up on his hands and knees to get on stage. He grabbed his guitar cord and stabbed the jack into his guitar right as everyone yelled, "One!" This deafening wail of feedback filled the venue. Jeff had barely made it. He completely nailed his solo on "Straight Up and Down." It was one of the moments that reminded us why we put up with him.

Everything was cool again. We did our last song, "Hyperventilation," which is really drone-y and long. Anton had started doing this thing where he'd take off his shirt and prowl the stage. He started doing this phallic stuff with the mic and eventually put it down his pants. When Oasis got on stage, Liam gets right up on the mic, almost putting his upper lip on it. We started cracking up because that was the same mic that had just been in Anton's pants. They had no idea what they had gotten into. They had cut up these huge, English coke lines with the super speed. The guitarist Paul "Bonehead" Arthur's jaw was grinding away like some kind of crank shaft.

If you watch the Oasis documentary *Supersonic*, they talk about the gig. Liam didn't go to sleep for three days. The next night they played Sacramento, and two nights later the Whiskey A Go-Go, and they just blew the whole show. The band broke up after that show because Liam was so cranked out. Noel quit and disappeared. He holed up in San Francisco with some chick he met. Eventually they found him, put the band back together, and finished the tour. As they say in the documentary, "After that, it was never the same." Noel never treated them the same after that. It was all because my friend got on that tour bus. If they had let me on, I could have warned them, "Don't do too much. This is crazy stuff!"

34

COURTNEY TAYLOR-TAYLOR

(The Dandy Warhols)

Featured alongside the Brian Jonestown Massacre in Dig! *were The Dandy Warhols, the somewhat less self-destructive side of that messy couple. Band leader Courtney Taylor-Taylor gives a harrowing account of the drug years along with a story about the time he came seconds away from shooting heroin for the first time with the Jonestown.*

It was a couple years ago that our guitarist Pete [Holmström] said to me, "I've seen you play fucked up before, but never so fucked up that you couldn't play guitar." We're usually all about the music and the feeling when we play live, but I literally couldn't play. This was in San Francisco, and I was forgetting where I was in the songs, and it was a mess. Some dude started playing tambourine on stage, and I thought it was Joel Gion from The Brian Jonestown Massacre. I'm like, "Hey, Joel!" I was so drunk that I couldn't see who it was. Turned out it was the bass player for The Warlocks.

It was the first time that I had all my winemaker friends come in from Napa for a show, and I didn't know you could get that fucked up just off wine. Wine's always been so good to me, and I'm a wine collector. My palette usually hits the wall at some point, and I have to stop drinking, because I'm not enjoying it. My friends had brought in all these amazing old wines, and there were about fourteen of us at this amazing restaurant, a block away from the venue.

I don't remember leaving the restaurant or getting on stage. I just remember mistaking the Warlocks dude for Joel, but that's the only thing I remember about the gig. A few days later in Sacramento, somebody who was at the San Francisco gig, said, "Man, it was awesome! I haven't seen you play fucked up like that in so long, and it made it super interesting." Jesus, man. Sometime around 1997, I got drunk in Brussels, and when I went on stage, I remember thinking, "I don't feel this at all. I don't feel anything." I was so drunk that I couldn't feel the music.

Usually, the feeling of playing and getting it going with the gang is like creating my own wave and surfing it with my best friends. I smoke weed and get stoned before every show, and that wave is an unbelievably powerful, emotionally cleansing experience. I'm literally shaking when I get on stage, but when we start going, that anxiety melts away, and we ride the wave. This time I wasn't feeling anything, and after the first song, some kid yelled really nasty, "You're drunk!" That was it, and I hadn't played drunk since the Independent show in San Francisco. I haven't played drunk since that one either. I don't feel music when I'm drunk, except for maybe something like, "Fight for Your Right to Party."

I remember a bunch of us going to a dance club in Madrid after a show. Great music, and I drank a bunch. The next bar was a small punk club, and I continued to drink. A friend of mine from Amsterdam said that later that night I was on the speaker box singing every line and dancing like a madman to "Fight for Your Right to Party." He said I didn't miss a line, and I thought that was so fucking weird. I had surely heard it a billion times, but I had never tried to sing along to it. Through osmosis, we all know that song. I think there's a ton of songs like that if you get drunk enough, you'll know every line. I probably know all the words to every campy, Bon Jovi mega-hit. I could probably crush "Dead or Alive" right now if I wanted to.

We used to play with The Brian Jonestown Massacre all the time. That lady [director Ondi Timoner] didn't really have a story, so she would get the Jonestown really whipped up about how nothing was happening for them while we were touring Europe. That led to them getting really jealous and angry, which ended up shaping the movie. She would trick us into doing shit, like going to the Jonestown house to shoot pictures when we had no idea the band wasn't going to be there. She convinced us that by shooting in this fucked-up house, it would help the Jonestown's career.

When she cut it together, it made us look like bad friends and icky people. She was constantly doing shit like that. Any time we were back in LA, which was rare, she would pack us all in a car and drive us out to the desert. On our day off, we had to drive four hours each way to the desert because Anton was out there shooting a video, and we had to be in it. We were constantly doing things that we didn't understand were made to make us look bad later.

It was really ugly, and we didn't get to be friends again with Jonestown for years after the documentary. We really couldn't say, "Dude! We did this because Ondi told us it would help you!" It would have sounded like the fucking lamest thing ever. So, we broke up as friends. Believe the movie if you want...we don't care anymore. Fuck off. Feelings were hurt on both sides, but we took Joel's band on tour. Our families hang out with Anton and his family when we're in Berlin. It's like we're finally adults and understand how everything went down. What a history we have— it's all part of rock legend now.

Ondi has the only footage of the Dandy's from back in the day, and she won't even let us see it. That's her M.O. It's what she does to people. She did the same thing to Russell Brand in a documentary she made about him. I don't think she feels confident enough to make something like a Tom Petty documentary, where there's hope and brightness. I think she felt no one would have watched *Dig!* if there wasn't constant ugliness and hatred. She's a bottom feeder. We lost about half our audience after the doc came out, and Jonestown would get shit thrown at them on stage as the crowd tried to antagonize Anton. People wanted to see a fight, and it made their lives miserable.

"Not If You Were the Last Junkie On Earth" was actually written about my ex-girlfriend, not The Brian Jonestown Massacre. Ondi convinced them it was about Anton. When I got back from the first Dandy's tour, my girlfriend had shot dope with the singer of my previous band. She showed up at my house looking like a drowned rat in the rain. She had a brown paper bag with her rig, some dope, and a king-size Snickers. She marched into my house and started chewing me out about what an asshole and weak man I was to break up with her. Then she shot up in my bathroom.

On a tour that I went on with the Jonestown, we had pulled over to get crap food at a mini-mart. I was on tour with them because I had been dumped by my girlfriend, and I was super depressed the whole time. There was a ton of drugs, and I was also staying really drunk, which made me more depressed. A bunch of the smack-heads from Jonestown, along with some of the people from the opening band decided to shoot up in the shitty mini-mart, somewhere in the Midwest.

I was so depressed that I went with them. They got out the needle, spoon, rubber tube, and smack. We were all piled into this disgusting bathroom stall, and I told them that I had never shot smack. I had smoked and snorted it but never shot. All it had ever made me do was lay on the sofa and vomit a lot, and I wasn't a big fan of the drug. At that point, I felt like "fuck it"—I'd do anything because I was so fucking depressed and constantly hungover.

Some dude tied me off, slapped my vein, and drew up the dope in the syringe, when we heard the door to the bathroom slam open. The owner yelled, "I don't know what the fuck you're doing in there, but you better get the fuck out right now. I'm calling the cops." I looked at that needle and my bulging vein. I undid the rubber tube and said, "Nope." We got out of there, and only later did it occur to me that the owner of that mini-mart could easily have saved my life. He saved my future. That's a really hard drug to come back from, and once you go down that road, it seems like you can't stop. You either have to die or become the one out of a thousand junkies that actually get free. I can count the ones I know on one hand.

I'm so fucking glad I didn't do it. I have enough fucking problems and garbage in my brain as a human being that I don't need that shit. I'm pretty full of self-loathing already. I don't need to go darker. I remember thinking that if I ever became successful, I'd come back and buy that mini-mart guy a car. That guy fucking saved my ass from a fate worse than death. Literally worse than death. I just found out that I love pills. I just got a Xanax prescription for my anxiety, but I have to make sure I don't do more than one a week. When I worry that my world is crashing, that I can't handle it, or that I'm going to fuck up the Dandy's and ruin my family, I'll do a quarter of a Xanax.

It's called expansion, and it's when your creative mind doesn't have any real skills to create its own barriers. It's what great artists are made of, but it's what fatalistic, self-abusing idiots are made of too, unfortunately. It's hard, because getting drunk is fun every single time for me. I'm not a mean or sad drunk. I'm a happy ass drunk. Like right now, I could start with the champagne, then move on to the whites and reds. Next thing you know, I want to invite people over. I'll call a guy and get a big pile of blow and have the crazy, rock 'n' roll scene again. I miss it, but then it's 5:00 a.m., and I'm super suicidally depressed. It would spiral into two or three consecutive days, and it's fucking gross.

It's hard to not want to go there, so I just stay busy. Idle hands....

35

SEAN YSEULT

(White Zombie)

As bassist for White Zombie, Yseult infiltrated the boys club of metal and quickly shut up any detractors with her amazing presence, precision, and kick-ass work ethic. She reminisces about getting pranked by the dearly departed Dimebag Darrell and spotlights the importance of mental and physical wellness.

White Zombie toured with Pantera a lot, and those guys are like brothers to me, especially Dimebag Darrell. He was always harassing me like a little sister, and he used to call me Junior, which became my nickname for all of Pantera. He was the best big brother you could have, and I was probably a couple years older than him! Not only was he the coolest guy in the world and my big bro, but he loved pulling pranks. Most bands, when you're on tour together, reserve the last day of the show for the pranks. For us, touring with Danzig and the Ramones, it wasn't easy to prank the bands I grew up worshipping. But we did it anyway. It's tricky, because you don't really want to fuck with Danzig. We covered the Ramones in silly string on stage, which was so silly and sophomoric. We definitely got the impression that Joey and Johnny were not into it.

Pranking was a daily affair for Dimebag, and the pranks were always amazingly creative, bizarre, and hilarious. He'd do something to the bus or walk onstage during our show like he was a janitor. You couldn't stop him. He especially liked to mess with me. One night he gave one of his roadies a ten-dollar bill and told him to go to the bank to get ten dollars' worth of pennies. I always wore these short and wide engineer boots with leggings. Halfway through our set, Darrell came out and poured all these pennies down my boots, during this intricate moment when I was standing still and doing some head spinning with my hair. I looked down, and he looked up smiling, pouring these pennies into my boots.

When he was done, it felt like it weighed a million pounds. I could barely move for the rest of the show. It was truly embarrassing, because it was in front of at least 10,000 people, and I'm known as someone that runs around onstage and puts on a show. The audience saw the whole thing, so they knew there was good reason that I couldn't move. I got off stage, and Darrell was waiting for me. He said, "Junior, did ya feel a little weighed down out there?"

He'd also dare people to do anything, especially his roadies. I had lime-green hair at one point, and he said, "Junior, I'll give you a hundred bucks if you cut off one of your locks." I cut it off, made a hundred bucks, and they gave it to their bus driver, who braided it into his hair. He walked around for days with this long, lime-green lock of hair attached to his head.

The craziest gig for me was back in the late eighties on one of our first tours. We were setting up our own shows, sleeping in a van, or on people's floors. We found these kids that wanted to set up a show. They had a really badass band called Doom Snake Cult, which is still one of the coolest band names ever. We drove out there and the two kids were like the stoner versions of Beavis and Butthead. They drove us out to Parumph, Nevada, in the middle of the desert. Our lodging was their trailer. They had set up the show outdoors, in a drainage ditch, where the locals go to shoot off their guns.

There we were in the desert with all these crazies who were hopped up on speed and shooting guns. To the guys' credit, they had gotten some gear and rigged up a PA system. We were just surrounded by sand, in this long ditch, wondering who was going to show up. Including us, Doom Snake Cult, and a few of their friends, there might have been fifteen people at that show. Everyone besides us was on acid, and they made a bonfire in front of us while we were playing. When the acid really kicked in, the kids started picking up the flaming logs and throwing them at each other, while these guns were firing all around us.

Over the years, I've had numerous people come up to me saying they were at that gig. Well, if you were actually one of the five people, great. Otherwise, no...you weren't. It was kind of like a weekend at Hunter Thompson's, and later in life, when we were selling out arenas, I looked fondly back on that gig. Everything becomes routine when you start playing sports arenas. It's all just concrete, with no real charm. You can't just walk outside and go to a cool restaurant or bar. It was so much different being in the van and actually hanging with bands. I'm not knocking selling out arenas, but it was a much different adventure before that happened.

On the first day of our tour with the Ramones, I was so excited that I got ready early so I could watch them. We were somewhere in North Dakota, and I went running up the stairs of the arena to get to the side stage. It was pitch black, and one of my legs fell through a hole in the stage. Someone had built it incorrectly and left out a board. My leg went straight through the stage, and my other leg snapped backwards, tearing my knee up.

It took me about two years to recover from that because we never stopped touring. I had to play the same night it happened, and I could barely stand. The worst thing for me is not being able to put on a good show. I got through it, but I don't remember how. I just wrapped it in an Ace bandage and went on. Somebody had called a "rock doctor" to bring me a couple painkillers, but it still hurt like hell. Throughout the tour, I kept seeing all these different doctors and getting larger leg braces. If you look up an old clip of us on David Letterman, I have a brace running from my ankle all the way up to my hip.

There's a whole team of people depending on you, and this is how touring musicians and athletes get hooked on painkillers and drugs. So much money is lost if the show or tour is cancelled. God forbid you get sick, as the show must always go on. Luckily, I didn't get hooked, because I've seen too much of that. We started out kind of straight-edge, and I have that mentality. I've never been dependent on drugs, but I had to take something. The rock doctors would show up, give me some Vicodin, and I'd take it. I don't really know if rock docs exist anymore, but they did back then. I never had a prescription, but if they showed up, I'd take one. None of it was handled very well.

I finally got surgery on my knee, but then I didn't have time to properly recover or go through physical therapy. I was right back on the road and was a mess for another couple of years. I'm still friends with Phil Anselmo from Pantera, and we talk about these old war stories all the time. He was in horrible pain for so long from performing, but he was the lead man, and the show had to go on. That's how this shit happens. It wasn't a surprise to hear about Tom Petty or Prince because I know about the road and the toll it takes on your body.

36

SAMMY HAGAR

(Van Halen)

Whatever your feelings on "Van Hagar," the Red Rocker has been doing it longer and harder than most. He explains why you should never try a mic stand throw without practice and what it's like to expose yourself to thousands of KISS fans at Madison Square Garden.

All of us rock stars are so fucking vain, especially when we're on our way up in the business. We're trying to become somebody and trying to be the coolest guy in the world, so that when shit goes wrong, it is really a bad feeling. Looking back, I'm able to laugh now, and I wish I could have handled both situations better. The first story was when I was in my first recording band, Montrose. It was my first time on a big stage, as I came from playing small clubs and backyard barbecues. When Montrose happened, it was a big jump for me. We made a record with Ted Templeman and toured the world.

We had a really good relationship with Bill Graham, and he gave us our first big shot. We played a couple clubs just to get our shit together, made a record, and then Bill puts us on at Winterland, opening for Humble Pie. I had a microphone stand that I had gold-plated with my advance money. I thought it was just the coolest thing in the world. I was a big fan of Rod Stewart, and I loved the way that he used to take his three-legged microphone stand, twirl it around, and throw it up in the air. I had never done that because I had never been on a big enough stage to try it. The ceiling where we used to rehearse wasn't even tall enough for me to jump fully in the air, so I had literally never even experimented with microphone stand acrobatics.

At soundcheck, day of the Winterland show, I didn't even practice my mic stand moves, but I knew I was going to do it during the show. We get on stage and, during the very first song, I flipped the fucking gold-plated mic stand into the air. The heavy end of it came right down on our bassist Bill Church's head, and it fucking knocked him out cold. I'm talking unconscious, with blood rushing down his face. The stand broke the headstock of his Fender bass, the instrument that had been on all the Van Morrison records.

I couldn't even sing because my voice was quaking so badly. We kept playing, but I was a stuttering wreck. Bill Graham was onstage with an icepack, icing down Church who was flat on his back. Graham was glaring at me with this look that said, "You goddamn fucking idiot." It was so humiliating that I couldn't have sex for six months after that. Honestly, it was one of those things where everybody was over it in no time, but not me. I was haunted. I'd be hanging out, lying in bed, walking down the street, or driving my car, and it would come back to me. I'd fucking cringe all over again.

Graham got Church all tightened up, got him another bass, and by the second song, Church was up and playing like nothing had happened. It wasn't until the third song that my voice had settled down, and I could actually attempt something like singing. It was brutal, and I never threw my mic stand again. That was my punishment for trying to copy Rod Stewart.

My other story is from 1977, and I had my second solo record out. KISS was starting a tour, and it was their first headlining show in New York, their hometown. They sold out Madison Square Garden, and they asked me at the last minute to be the opening act for the ten-show, East Coast run. Gene Simmons and Paul Stanley were both fans of Montrose, and they liked my first solo record. I go on stage to open Madison Square Garden, but nobody knew who I was, or even that I was on the bill, because I was added last minute. I didn't even have any fans yet anyway.

"Ladies and gentlemen, please welcome Sammy Hagar!" The place immediately starts fucking booing. I was still green from Montrose, and I didn't feel like I was anywhere near famous, so I just tried kicking as much ass as I could. During the third song, which was a Donovan-balled cover called, "Catch the Wind," people started flipping me off and really losing their shit. I was looking out at the crowd, and I stopped the song. I yelled, "You fucking assholes! You didn't even give me a chance. You started booing me before hearing the music. Fuck you!"

Everybody in the audience was dressed up like KISS. As far as I could see, they had all the makeup on too. Since it was New York, I said, "I see they've flown in an audience from Los Angeles for this show." That really pissed them off, and they started throwing cups at me. I pulled down my pants, dropped my drawers, and pulled out my dick. I shook it at the crowd, then smashed my 1961 Stratocaster to pieces, and walked offstage.

Gene and Paul were standing backstage, as they had heard all the commotion and wanted to know what the fuck was going on. Bill Graham, God bless him, was in New York on his way to the airport. He heard on the radio that I had been added to the KISS show, so he had told the driver to turn around and take him to the show. So he's backstage and had just walked in during my meltdown. He's shaking his head, and his hand is covering his face. Gene and Paul were doing the exact same thing.

I unloaded on them, too, saying, "Fuck you guys too!" And that was it. I didn't do any more shows with KISS. I stomped away to my dressing room. Paul was saying, "You can't talk to people like that, man! You gotta go out and prove yourself. You can't do it like that." I'm still going, "Fuck you and your makeup and your fans!" Bill Graham was in my face, but I was furious.

That night almost made me want to quit the business. It was humiliating and disheartening, and my poor band didn't know what to do. One of the guys, my rhythm guitarist who was the newest to the band, quit after that show.

Those are the two most embarrassing moments in my career. After that, things got pretty good. I never had that much hard luck, and I learned how to win over hostile audiences. As for my Jim Morrison, whipping-out-my-dick moment, I didn't get in any trouble. Hell, it was New York, and they don't care. They see that every day. Jim fucked up because he did it in Florida.

37

PAUL HARTNOLL

(Orbital)

Brothers Phil and Paul Hartnoll were fathers of the early UK rave scene and are one of the most enduring sibling partnerships (save for a short split in the 2000s). This is also the only chapter to prominently feature a waterslide.

This one was painfully awful. In 1996, we were touring Europe, and for some reason, we weren't popular in Germany, and I don't know why. They like their techno music, but they didn't care for us. We got an offer to play a gig by a rich kid whose father owned a resort somewhere in the Black Forest. We arrived, and there was this beautiful, rotund restaurant space, but the kid didn't want us to play there. He said to us, "I've got a great idea for where I want you to play."

He led us down to this massive swimming pool with two really tall waterslides connected to a gigantic tower. He pointed at the tower and said, "That's where I want you to play." We agreed, as it was a nice, sunny day with lovely weather. It really was a massive tower, and we had to lug all the gear to the top, which was a real chore. We had these blunderbuss, analog synths that didn't take well to European power, so we couldn't use those. I spent most of the day trying to reprogram the synths, so it was shaping up to be a really unpleasant, stressful day.

Everybody went off to dinner, and I was stuck with the goddamn synths on top of the tower. I finally managed to get some dinner in the lovely, round restaurant building, and all I could think about was how much I'd rather be playing in there. The waiter told me that it was asparagus season and that I had to try it. He came back with this horrendously over-boiled asparagus and an awful cup of tea. I left, hoping that some of the crowd would have arrived by then. I kept waiting and waiting, but no one was showing up. When we were set to play, to say that twenty-five people were there would have been excessive.

As we were getting ready to play, the sky absolutely clouded over with really ominous, black storm clouds. At that point, I decided I'd had enough and started drinking, which is not something I'd normally do. Occasionally, I'd have a nip of vodka before going on, but this time I was properly having a drink. I kinda staggered up the tower again, and we started playing, with the synths still broken. I never got them fixed after all that time.

We were playing for the twenty-five people below, hanging around the swimming pool. Way up on the tower, it was like we were playing to nobody. We watched as thunder and lightning rolled in from the distance. It seemed to be the exact height as our tower and was hitting these pylons a few fields away. My bandmate Phil started nudging me, saying that we needed to get down immediately.

I was drunk and starting to feel like Dr. Frankenstein at that point. I started yelling at Phil, "I'm going to finish this fucking gig if it kills me! I'm not fucking quitting now!" We were playing our track "The Box," which is kind of gothic anyway. I'm still ranting, and I had brought a plastic bucket up there for a toilet, because I was so sick of climbing down the fucking tower to use a proper restroom. Since I was drinking, I was peeing in the bucket during the show, and I accidentally knocked it over.

At that point, it was about as bad as it could get, and then we started getting pelted with rain. It was pouring down on the equipment, even though we had a small roof over our heads. Phil finally grabbed me by the shoulders and said, "You've got to get the fuck off this tower. You're going to get hit by lightning." He had to drag me down the thing, kicking and screaming. They finally pulled the plug on it when we got to the bottom of the tower.

When we finally got all the gear down, the weather turned nice and peaceful again. We left all bedraggled, wet, and tired. We walked into the lovely, rotund building, and found a room full of people with a separate gig going on. It was transformed into a really nice little club. We were thinking, "Where the fuck is that little idiot who put us up on the fucking tower?" Here was this brilliant place, and he had stuck us on the back end of his land, where no one even knew we were playing.

It wasn't like there wasn't room for our gear in there or anything; we obviously could have played inside. Thankfully, we didn't get hassled from the rich kid about quitting early. After all, I bet it wasn't his money anyway. He was actually a sweet guy, just a little daft. I think he was quite horrified by what had happened.

Being in a band with my brother hasn't always been a bed of roses. Thirty years of working with any one person is going to be difficult, but thirty years of working with my brother, who is four years older, gets really annoying. I think we've gotten off lightly when I look at the in-fighting between the Kinks, Oasis, or even Dire Straits. Look at UB40! God almighty! They're still at each others' throats. Those are my cautionary tales, and I've always told myself, "Don't end up in those situations."

38

MARK FOSTER

(Foster the People)

Here's something that will make you feel old: "Pumped Up Kicks" is approaching its ten-year anniversary! I figured we needed some input from an act that wasn't active in the '90s, so here's band leader Mark Foster on the terror that any serious, young band must face: the "big break" show.

When thinking about this book and what I would share, my mind immediately went back to the first time Foster the People played Coachella. It was in 2011, before our first record, *Torches*, had even come out. The public had only heard three songs of ours at that point, with "Pumped Up Kicks" being the one that took off. We were on our first US tour, and Coachella was the final show. We were only playing to three hundred or five hundred capacity rooms, so Coachella looming at the end was already daunting. We had no crew, only a monitor guy who ran front-of-house sound, and a tour manager, who would help us load gear.

I had been going to Coachella since 2003 so, for me, it was a really big deal personally. It was gonna be a hometown crowd, with my friends and family in the audience. It's an incredible rite of passage to play Coachella, especially if you're from the West Coast. It was also our first time playing any festival. When we showed up and I looked out into the tent, it was completely packed, with people flooding out into the fairgrounds. There must have been 15,000 people there. The most people I'd ever been on stage in front of might have been 700 tops. The whole band had experience being on stage but not at that level. It was terror, exhilaration, and a million other feelings coming out at once.

The main thing that freaked me out, apart from the crowd, was the simple fact that we weren't ready. When we started and I put "Pumped Up Kicks" online for free, I wasn't thinking that far ahead, even though I had been playing music my whole life. While I had been building toward this Coachella moment, I couldn't have felt more unprepared.

I was pacing backstage, and before we went on, I looked out at the crowd and saw Clint Eastwood, David Hasselhoff, and Usher all talking to each other. I thought, "What kind of fucking weird movie am I in?" David Hasselhoff and Usher walk into a bar...it's like the setup to a joke. Management, our label, and my girlfriend at the time were all there, and I told them all to get away from me. I walked out the back of the tent and sat with my back against the fence. I meditated, and went into a full visualization of how the show would go down.

There was only a twenty-minute changeover between bands, so without a proper crew, we were gonna have to hustle because we had a lot of gear. YouTube was live-streaming our show, and the band before us went long, which cut into our changeover time. We ended up going on about twenty minutes late, but the YouTube stream had been going the whole time, and it was this mad cluster-fuck of us trying to set up our gear. The Coachella house guys were helping, but I couldn't go out yet—I was still sitting with my back against the fence, trying to find my happy place so I wouldn't have a full-on panic attack.

People were shouting at me that we had to go on, and I remember thinking, "What would Michael Jordan do?" I sat up and called my bandmates over. I said, "Look guys, don't let the crowd see you sweat. Let's walk out there, smile, and have a blast. We don't have to kill it, and even if everything goes to shit, we just have to survive." That was my thinking, because nobody had really seen us live at that point. Nobody knew what we were made of, and this was the first time that music journalists and the world would be seeing us live.

First impressions—for any artist—are so important. Walking out onto the stage, all I kept thinking was, "We're not ready... we're not ready...we're not ready." The crowd roared, but it was like an out-of-body experience. We opened with the song "Warrant," which is the last song on *Torches*. Before every band started using toms, I'd like to emphasize that we were doing it. Me and our drummer Mark Pontius would both play this tribal drum beat intro before I would throw my sticks and jump behind the piano, hitting the first chord of the song.

We were pounding the drums, and everything was going fine. But when I hit my first chord on the piano, I couldn't hear a thing.

The piano was not in my monitors at all, and the people running the festival monitors had no idea what our record sounded like. They didn't know which parts needed to be loud, or have any idea what the proper balance should be. My piano was super low, and Pontius's snare sounded like somebody flicking a piece of cardboard twenty feet away. It was just nothing, and the piano is the instrument that grounds where my vocals rest.

Our first fucking song, in front of all these people, and this was just about the worst thing that could have possibly happened. I played the entire song just by watching the note patterns of my hands. I could hear the bass guitar, so I did my best to sing along to that. I didn't freak out, and I don't really remember what happened after the first song, but I remember closing with "Pumped Up Kicks" and the whole crowd singing along and clapping.

Walking off that stage, with everyone giving us love, was the first time I had ever felt that validation. It was the sensation of surviving trial by fire and living to tell about it. We didn't kill it, that's for sure. But we survived, and that's all I really wanted. If we had fucked that show up, we might have been done. Career over. As a band, we might have been done before anything had really started. The blogosphere was maturing in 2011, and I can't imagine what artists have to go through now. Even back then, Twitter had just started. Instagram was something I had only been hearing about in whispers. The days of doing something embarrassing and having it plastered all over the internet in ten minutes, weren't there yet. Thank God.

I feel really lucky that we still have a career and that things are still working. When "Pumped Up Kicks" got so big, and because we had no foundation at the time, we did every interview, every in-store, and every radio morning show. I felt we needed to work three times as hard to show the world that we weren't just this one song. It was really stressful because I moved to LA when I was eighteen and had been a starving artist up to that point. "Pumped Up Kicks" started to happen when I was twenty-six, so it was eight years of sleeping in my car and delivering pizzas.

I was over being a barista and never having any savings in the bank. My mom gave me a 1993 Toyota Camry that I drove from Ohio to LA. It was so beat up by the end, and I had logged over 350,000 miles on it. I drove that thing around LA for four years with no A/C and two broken windows that were duct taped. In the middle of summer, my driver-side window wouldn't roll down. Then the muffler broke, so the car became insanely loud. The California emissions are so strict that I had to bribe an emissions guy to pass my car.

If I had lost my car, I would have had no way to make money. My car was loud as fuck after the muffler kicked. You could hear me coming six blocks away, and it was so embarrassing. When all my dreams were coming true, it was exciting, but it was also "*don't fuck this up!*" Coachella was our shot, and it didn't come when I wanted it to, but I had to take it. I would have loved six months with the band playing shows and getting really comfortable. We just had to put our heads down and make it happen.

Here's a quick, fun one. We were in Minneapolis at the 7th St Entry, the smaller room of First Ave. It was the weekend, and playing Minneapolis on a weekend is pretty nuts. It gets lit, and our keyboardist Isom Innis was set up on the edge of the stage.

He suddenly felt this thing in his butt, in the middle of a song. I saw him jump, and he turned around to see two women giggling. It looked like a mother and daughter. The older woman was somewhere around fifty-five, and the daughter was around twenty. He started playing again and felt the same butt sensation again a couple minutes later.

He kept scooting in closer to the stage, as he began to realize that the cougar was fingering his butt. The third time it happened, she stuck her hand all the way down his pants and fingered his butthole. At that point, he yelled, "Whoa! Are you fucking kidding me?" All the guy wanted to do was play music and not screw it up, and he was suddenly forced to do battle with a butthole-obsessed cougar. We finished the show, and as I got off the stage dripping sweat, I grabbed a cold tall boy. I was drinking the beer, cooling down, and this sixty-year-old guy with gray hair grabbed my beer and started chugging it in front of my face.

The guy was pretty big and ex-military looking and wore a white shirt with a sheriff's badge logo on it. After he finished, he slammed the can down and wandered onto the stage. We were in the process of loading up our gear, and the fucking guy fell into our drum kit, knocking the whole thing over. This was a few shows before Coachella, and our tour manager, who is an ex-rugby player, grabbed the guy. "Alright mate, you've had enough," he said, as he dragged the dude away. We were dying laughing the whole time because I cycled from being scared, to confused, to amusement. I think Isom was just happy to get out of there quickly after being violated.

39

GENESIS P-ORRIDGE

(Throbbing Gristle/Psychic TV)

Arguably the creators of industrial music, Throbbing Gristle were far more concerned with the deconstruction of music and live performance than delivering cohesion, and gender-neutral P-Orridge, suffering with leukemia, reflects on the entire journey.

I was a huge fan of Brian Jones, and I grew up buying every Rolling Stones single the day it came out. Then he was murdered, and I went to see the "new" Rolling Stones in Hyde Park on July 5th, 1969. There were half a million people there, and it's still the worst show I've ever seen. It was impossible to get anywhere near the stage, and we were way back in the trees. When they started playing, it was so fucking shambolic that people started leaving. Within twenty minutes, I was able to walk to the very front of the stage.

They had boxes of white butterflies that they released to symbolize Brian's rising to heaven. All the boxes had been left in the hot sun, and almost all of them died. The roadies were chucking them into the air to make it look like they were flying. It was really gross and embarrassing. If you see video footage of the show, it doesn't show how many people walked away in disgust. There's a deathbed confession by the foreman who was working on Jones's house, and he admitted he killed him. He had grown to hate Brian Jones because Jones treated him like shit. He got sick of it one night and held Brian under water until he died.

The first real rock gig Throbbing Gristle ever did was supporting Hawkwind, featuring a young Lemmy Kilmister, at Bradford, St. Georges Hall in 1971. It was a benefit for hippies who had been caught smuggling hash, and I was already into my "anti-rock" music ideas. I brought a dwarf with me to play lead guitar, who'd never played before that night. We had Cosey Fanni Tutti dressed as a schoolgirl, strutting around and firing a starter pistol in the air. Our singer was a surfer from Bridlington who stood on a surfboard atop a bucket of water on stage.

Everyone was getting into bigger and better drum kits at the time, like Pink Floyd, who had a huge setup. For my drum kit, we just took a bunch of stuff and piled it together. The performance was the guy on the surfboard making up lyrics, the dwarf trying to get sounds out of his guitar, the gun going off, and me piling drums and cymbals into this massive mess that couldn't possibly be played. It was like twenty drums, and I sat down in the middle of it all, throwing expanded, polystyrene granules in the air like snow. That was the show! The hippies were completely baffled and silent the entire time.

In the mid '90s, I got a phone call from Nik Turner of Hawkwind, asking if I wanted to perform on a tour with the band. I agreed to be keyboard sampler and did three West Coast dates with Nik. We were in the dressing room the night of the first show, and I said to him, "You probably won't remember this, but we actually did a gig supporting you in 1971." Nik said, "You were the one with the snow! You fucking jammed all of our effects pedals!" He told me it took them ages to clean them out and get them working again.

The first Throbbing Gristle record was an indie album, released in 1977, called *Second Annual Report*. We were the first to put out an album without a label. Side Two was a film soundtrack, which was one long twenty-three minute track called "After Cease to Exist." When you watch the movie, you get the title, and then it's blank, which is actually black film. The music keeps going, but there's nothing to watch. After ten minutes, when you're thinking, "Oh God, this is one of those weird, experimental films," there's suddenly five minutes of imagery, which included a fake castration of our bandmate Chris Carter.

Our other bandmate Peter "Sleazy" Christopherson was part of the Casualties Union, and they were a group of performers that would act injured or have fits for authorities who were practicing for emergencies. He was taught how to make incredibly realistic cuts and blood, and we did a fast-edit cut of fake castration. We thought everyone would realize it was obviously fake, but lots of people thought it was real. It upset a lot of people but, thankfully, no one tried to have us arrested for showing a snuff film.

The weirdest Throbbing Gristle gig was when we were invited to play for the students at the Architectural Association in London. In the early days, we tried to tailor each gig for the venue—to do something different every time. One time we found a bunch of huge mirrors made of mylar that we put across the front of the stage, so all the audience could see were reflections of themselves. Another thing we liked to do was put halogen lamps across the front of the stage. We'd turn them on full blast so the audience was blinded and couldn't see anything.

For the Architectural Association, we were trying to come up with something uniquely architectural that we could do for a stage. There was a triangular yard between three buildings at the Association, and we built a twenty-foot cube of scaffolding that we covered in tarps. We put all our instruments inside, and we put our PA system flat on the ground, pointing straight up. We had cameras inside the cube operating on closed-circuit TV because we noticed there were TVs all through the Architectural Association.

When we went to play, if you wanted to see what we were doing, you had to stay in the building and look at the TV monitors, but there was no sound feed. If you wanted to hear what we were doing, you had to go upstairs and hang outside a window, or go onto the roof and look down. The students went nuts, and there was a riot. They smashed down a door into the yard, and somebody actually ripped out a toilet, and dropped it down from the roof. Luckily, it hit the scaffolding and didn't kill anyone.

It was a remarkable example of a really unexpected response. They were furious and enraged that they couldn't see and hear the performance at the same time. They wanted a proper show. It got really scary as the students were hurling down all kinds of crap onto us. We weren't into shocking people—it was always about the reaction. That's what was interesting to us—breaking down the traditional structure of what people consider a rock 'n' roll show.

With Throbbing Gristle, none of us were trained musicians. We all agreed that we never wanted to become a traditional rock band, and we wanted to create something new and different. We wanted to constantly evolve. Our basic methodology—one we still use today—is to decide on a project, then strip away everything we don't need or can't have. That's how we created industrial music, which was through a process of reduction. We were doing it because we were curious, and we decided that we liked the sounds we were making. We jammed every weekend for the whole of 1975. Our first album was recorded on cassettes, and it broke the old rock-and-roll system.

It was the idea that anyone can be in a band, and anyone can create fascinating music. You can create any emotion you want to express without knowing how to play. Those glue-sniffers the Ramones said to learn three chords and start a band. My answer to that was why learn any chords at all? Drugs never played into our creative process. We had our '60s psychedelic experiences, but during the Throbbing Gristle time period, we didn't do any drugs. It's ironic that we had this really decadent image in the public eye, but we were really as pure as the driven snow.

The makeup of our audience was mostly eccentric punks. The first concert TG did was in a pub for twenty people. The local newspaper reviewed the show, and I'll never forget the headline: "Even an ape with severed arms could play the bass guitar better than Genesis." Isn't that great? I wear it as a badge of honor. We also discovered orgone accumulators around that time. Orgone is that beautiful smell after a lightning strike in a storm. It's negative ions that produce that smell, and it's poorly labeled because negative ions are good for you. Positive are bad.

We got an electrician we knew to build us a giant negative-ion generator. It took huge voltage, and it was very dangerous. It had a grill of wires in the front, and a fan that blew the ions through. When it was on stage, we put out a sign that read, "Do Not Touch. *This can kill you!*" Of course, people tried to put their fingers in it. It would crackle, and blue sparks would fly everywhere. It was amazing. I wish I still had it.

In TG, we only ever played for sixty minutes. We had a digital clock on stage, and no matter where we were in a song or improvisation, we stopped immediately. We never did encores because it felt like another rock 'n' roll cliché that we weren't interested in following. One of the first TG shirts I wore read: Rock and Roll is for Ass Lickers. I wrote on my guitar: This Machine Kills Music. We hated when live bands sounded just like their albums.

One reason TG stopped was that our shows were beginning to feel regimented. They stopped being loose, and we didn't want to be one of those bands that toured all the time, like Pink Floyd. We were just starting to get recognition, but we didn't want bigger and bigger audiences. We didn't want hit records. We wanted to change the fucking world.

The most outrageous moment in my career was probably a Psychic TV show at Thee Mean Fiddler in 1989. We were doing our rave-era music and had a great arrangement with certain venues, where they would turn a blind eye to the psychedelic aspect of what we were doing. We had friends that had access to quite a good amount of psychedelics and MDMA. They'd come to concerts and give it away for free. That night at Mean Fiddler, I decided to experiment with chemicals during the concerts. I dressed in three different outfits to match each drug I took.

One was a pair of white pajamas, that under blacklight read, "Yes." Under normal light it read, "No." The next was a very psychedelic, flower-child jacket under the pajamas. The other was just a gray, nondescript shirt. Every third of the way through the concert, I took a different drug. We played for about six hours, so every two hours, it was a different drug and different outfit. The first drug was MDMA, which was very high-grade, pharmaceutical ecstasy. The next was magic mushrooms, followed by LSD tabs.

There's a video of the show, and there's an amazing moment with a close-up of my face, with my eyes rolled back in my head. You can only see the whites of my eyes, and I look like a zombie. The anchor was the music, and we had a following at the time of people who would get naked and dance on stage. They were all going mad, doing weird dances in the nude. My daughter Caresse was there, dancing with her mum. It was a fantastic, beautiful experience.

When it was over, we packed up, but I was still completely out of my tree. We walked out to the cars and realized that none of us were capable of driving. I certainly couldn't, as I was way out there. People started shouting, "I can't! I'm on acid!" Or, "I can't! I'm still rolling!" When all was said and done, it was decided that I was the safest one to drive, and I drove everyone home. One by one. I'd say to the person in the passenger seat, "Tell me if the light is green or red." By some miracle, I got everyone home safe.

There was a point where I stopped learning anything with drugs, and I put them down. I've got leukemia now, and I'm fighting to stay alive. The last thing on my mind is tripping. I get tired very easily now, which is normal with leukemia. My kidneys completely failed a few months back, which was really scary. I was in the ICU, and they stuck a tube into my jugular vein, which went into a dialysis machine. I just had to lie there, with this thing sucking my blood out, cleaning it, and putting it back. I was incredibly close to death, and I'm only sixty-eight.

What's important to me now is getting as much done before I'm not here. I do what I do, whether or not the outside world gets it. People trust me to be honest, and that will always warm my heart.

DAVID YOW

(Jesus Lizard)

While writing this book, I'd occasionally post on social media, "What art-
ists should I include?" David Yow was unanimously the most requested, and
he didn't disappoint. He probably holds the record for "Most Naked" in the
book too.

We played Salt Lake City one time, in a pretty large room that
was about 1,000 capacity, and only three people showed up. It was
a drunk Native American, a drunk frat boy, and some other dude.
The Native American and the frat boy heckled us between songs.
It was the most humiliating thing I've ever experienced on stage.
It was the only time, over the course of thousands of Jesus Lizard
shows, that I turned to the guys and said, "You want to just stop?"
But we played the whole show for those three assholes.

One time we played England, and I had taken off one of my
boots and put it on the mic stand. I was really broke at the time,

and those were the only shoes I had. Some skinhead jumped on stage and threw my boot into the crowd. I knocked him down and started punching him in the back of the head. Remember the show *Twin Peaks*—the original one—where Bob comes crawling over the couch? As I was punching the skinhead, I looked up and this long-haired guy that looked just like Bob came crawling over the barricade. It looked like it was in slow motion, and it was the skinhead's buddy coming at me. I thought I was doomed. Right before he got to me, our roadie came out of the blue and laid the guy out. It was fucking incredible. I broke my hand from punching the back of the guy's head. Fortunately, I got my boot back.

Our audience was extremely varied. I don't think we attracted much of a hardcore audience because we were too arty and weird for them. Drugs weren't really our thing, but alcohol? Uh...yeah! We would drink all day long, every day. We'd finish a case, then get another. At our shows, alcohol was a pretty important member of the band. There were a few times when I would overdo it and be embarrassed, which led to a talking-to from the band. There was a show in Arizona where the reviewer wrote, "David Yow now owes me twenty dollars." There's a live video of us playing "Glamorous" at CBGB, which was night fifteen of fifteen nights in a row. You can see we're all exhausted but also completely wired on speed. You can see me grinding my teeth in the video. None of us were ever junkies or shit like that. At our reunion shows, the rule was no bourbon before showtime.

I don't know what the percentage is exactly, but I'd say I was naked on stage 20 percent of the time. I saw the Cramps back in 1979, and Lux had fallen into the audience. As he was climbing back onstage, somebody yanked his pants down. He finished the set with this pants around his ankles, and I thought, "That's so cool!" I was pretty tight with the Butthole Surfers, and a lot of times, Gibby would end up in only boxer shorts, and those would sometimes come off. On the only West Coast tour Scratch Acid ever did, we played Seattle, and it was crazy sold out. For some reason, Seattle really gave a shit about Scratch Acid. During the first song, a guy pantsed me. I decided to be cool about it and finish the song. I noticed there were a group of girls elbowing each other, giggling and pointing at my dick. It was so small, like just the head without the dick. I talked to my bass player after, and he said, "Don't worry. Girls know dicks are like accordions."

That was the first time I was naked, so it technically started with Scratch Acid. I honestly don't know why I decided to do that with the Jesus Lizard. Many times it wasn't my fault and a situation where the crowd undressed me. Most of the time it was me thinking, "Well, I don't need these clothes anymore!" I obviously have some exhibitionist tendencies, but if I was being psychoanalyzed, I don't know how I would explain it. We played the Roxy in Los Angeles, and after I got naked, this girl in the front row kept feeling my dick while we were playing. I put my hand down her pants and started fingering her. Because she was so close to the stage, I don't think anyone could see what was happening. She just stared at me the whole time. She wasn't smiling, and that's as close as I ever got to sex onstage. That one was pretty intense and sleazy.

I got arrested in Cincinnati once for public nudity. I had dropped my pants at a show, and a friend came over and said, "The D.A. is in the audience, and they said that if you do it again, you're gonna get arrested." I didn't do it again, but after the show, two cops came backstage and put me in handcuffs anyway. They took me downtown. These cops were such fucking assholes. They kept saying, "Oh man, this is great! We haven't had a rock star in here since Ted Nugent!" I get offended if somebody calls me a rock star. They made me take off my earrings and wedding ring. I yelled at them, "What? Am I gonna tunnel out of here with my fucking wedding ring?"

I was detained for a couple hours and ended up with a fine. A couple of the cops asked for my autograph, and I wrote, "Fuck you, David Yow." I went back to the venue, and Sonic Youth was finishing up. I was backstage talking to our manager about the situation, and Courtney Love plopped herself down on a table. She mumbled, "Aww man, I don't know what the problem is! I showed my cooch, and they didn't fucking arrest me, man!" I had to show up in court a few months later in Hamilton County. Everybody who went before me was charged with domestic violence. It was all these wife-beating motherfuckers, and when they called me up and read, "David Yow, for recklessly and willingly exposing his private parts," everybody looked at me like I was Satan. It's OK to beat your wife, but don't show your dick! They fined me 400 bucks, and I couldn't go to Hamilton County for a year. Big fucking bummer, right? Nobody likes Cincinnati anyway.

I've never wished we were more popular or that we had broken through to the mainstream. I'm completely happy with what we did. I have famous friends who can't even go to the grocery store without being recognized. I'd be OK with being rich, but I think fame is a curse. The reunion shows were a lot of fun, and people said we were better now than the old days. Money was never the reason that we made music. I was worried that, in some way, we did the reunion shows for the money. I thought people were placating me by saying, "If nothing else, you're making a lot of people happy." And that's true. To look out and see those smiling faces—it's really cool.

41

DAVE PIRNER

(Soul Asylum)

While forever remembered for "Runaway Train," Soul Asylum shared the punk "Fuck it!" spirit of fellow Minnesotans The Replacements. Never comfortable in the mainstream, front man Pirner was more comfortable fighting audience members than appearing on MTV.

This is so hard for me to do, because there's such a shitshow of memories that I've suppressed. There were so many things that went wrong that I've tried to forget, but there's also the "look back and laugh" factor, which is a good thing for keeping sane. Twenty years ago, that shit wasn't funny at all. One thing that immediately comes to mind was a gig we played in Iowa City at a bar called Amelia's in the early '90s. It was a punk show, and everyone was slamming around. We were playing most excellently, of course, and someone threw a lit cigarette at me, which bounced off my face. I saw who did it, and I saw red. I flew off the stage and wrestled the dude to the ground.

It was an immediate reaction, which was *kill*. I tossed my guitar and attacked. Chaos erupted, and it turned into this huge hog pile. We were sitting backstage after the gig, and I was still pissed off. I'm grumbling to the band, "Who the fuck throws a lit cigarette?" This woman came into the dressing room, and said, "I'm so sorry about the kid that threw the cigarette. It was my son." Turned out, she owned the bar. Then, she pulled out the biggest bag of cocaine I've ever seen in my life. She said, "Maybe this will make you feel better" and handed it to me. My only thought was, "This is a weird fucking life that I've chosen."

It was very chaotic when we did gigs with The Replacements. We were two bands that would drink any other band under the table. During the Bob Stinson days, there was a lot of hilarity and irreverence. The attitude was, "We don't give a fuck. Where's the beer?" I still have that attitude, and I've never really grown out of it. Even in the MTV days, we had that punk attitude and wouldn't put up with bullshit. We wanted to do everything our way and wouldn't let anyone tell us what to do. It became a challenge as we were increasingly asked to do more things. I never really knew where to draw the line because people are always amused by tom-foolery and debauchery. We didn't give a shit about anything, but we still had to do the job. We still wanted to play our music and not fuck it up.

People start to talk, and when you get a reputation for being crazy people, that doesn't really help. I can't name names for this story, but we were playing the 9:30 Club in Washington, D.C., back when it was the old 9:30 Club. We were playing a show with some good friends of ours, and one of the band members had some coke. I wasn't aware because no one had offered me any. However, one of the guys in my band did a big, fat line, and about three minutes into our set, he turned to me and said, "Uhh...that wasn't coke." I'm like, "What's going on? How do you feel." His eyes were glazed and he muttered, "I don't know...I don't know." I think it was the first and last time he had ever done a big line of heroin. He was so disoriented that it was kinda funny. Man, get a roadie to test that shit!

This one still makes me cringe. We were playing a huge festival in Holland called Pink Pop. It was the biggest crowd we had ever experienced. These festivals happen all the time now in America, but back in the early '90s, it was a European phenomenon. There was one of those ramps that extends into the crowd, which we called the "ego ramp." I'm not the lead guitarist, but for this gig, we decided I'd have a solo. I'm psyching myself up, as we were just a little punk band from Minnesota. I'm thinking, "I'm gonna walk out on that ego ramp and just rip this solo." It was a long ramp, and right when I get to the end where I'm gonna rip this amazing solo for Holland the cord comes out of the guitar. I'm standing on this ramp, thinking I'm some guitar God, with no power coming out of my instrument.

When I realized what had happened and I turned to the band, they were all laughing at me. I was completely isolated on that ego ramp, thinking, "Well...so much for this gig." I did the slow walk of shame back down the ramp and walked straight off stage. It got to be a grind, where we'd go to Paris and play "Runaway Train" on five different TV shows in one afternoon. It was very alienating. It's not a song that is difficult for me to play, thankfully. It was way out of my range or something like that, things would have sucked a lot more.

We stopped playing it. We did a whole tour where it wasn't in the set. We ended up putting it back in because I started getting the whole, "We drove all the way from Alaska and just wanted to hear one song, and you guys didn't play it." I started to think how stupid our refusal to play it was. Why not just play the goddamn thing? One night the booking manager from First Avenue in Minneapolis, who had seen us play eight million times, came backstage with his new baby. He said, "My baby and I were listening to "Runaway Train," and it was such a special moment." At that point, I realized it wasn't really my song anymore. It really meant something to people.

I remember seeing a guy in a pub once that was playing traditional Irish songs by request on guitar. He had a little sign that read, "Danny's Song. $10." He got requested that song so much that he was completely sick of playing it. I began to think that I should wear a "Runaway Train" sign around my neck. I'm past all that. Now, it's just another three minutes and forty-five seconds out of my life. I can handle it. I'm calloused to touring now. So much has gone wrong over the years that I still want to laugh and cry at the same time. But I still love it so much. Once we're locked in and playing, I'm comfortable. The rest of it still sucks.

42

STEPHAN JENKINS

(Third Eye Blind)

Growing up a '90s kid, "Semi-Charmed Life" is still one of my favorite songs, so I had to get Jenkins for the book. The final paragraph, in my mind, is pure poetry and the best summation of the spirit of this project.

Whenever I'm the keynote speaker at some kind of music writing seminar, I'll inevitably get the question: "How do you make it?" Whenever they ask, I always say, "I never asked that question." Musicians don't dress, talk, or live the same as normal people. You have to be a bit insane to do it for a living. Before I had a record deal, I was always hustling to get a band together. I'd get one going, hold it together for a minute, and then it would fall apart. Everyone would turn out to be a drug addict, or they'd break off for some other band, and it was really hard for me to get a gig. A buddy and I just decided that we were gonna put on our own gig. This was in San Francisco, and there was a festival called Noise Pop. There was no way we were gonna get in because I could never count on any one band member to show up for practice.

So, a friend and I decided to make our own festival. He had access to a copier, so we stole posters and made one up. It was a picture of his girlfriend in pigtails smoking a cigarette, but she had stuck her belly out with her shirt pulled up, so she looked pregnant. It was a great shot! We decided we'd be the anti-Noise Pop. We called the fest Cocky Pop and made up these PSAs, which I snuck into the local radio station Live 105. They actually put them on air, so I stole airtime. I rented space, we worked on songs, and invited other bands to play the fest. I worked my hands raw putting up posters all over the city.

The big day arrived, and my friend never showed up. He was the drummer of our two-piece, so I had nothing. After all that work, and years of trying to get a band going, I was described as sitting ashen and shaky on the floor. That incident set my musical trajectory back a year, where I went back to the musical jail of trying to get something going. I didn't play a show for another year and a half. That's how much that one fucked me up. The point of me telling this story is that at no point during that night, or any time after, did I ever consider quitting. That's why when someone asks me what it takes to make it, I seriously doubt they're going to make it. No sane person would willingly put themselves through the amount of suffering it takes to make it.

The first time Third Eye Blind played Japan was at the Fuji Rock Festival, and we got hit with a typhoon. It was us, Foo Fighters, and Red Hot Chili Peppers. We were playing at the base of Mt. Fuji when it hit. Stinging rain was blowing sideways into our faces as we were playing. I was so new and still young enough that I just thought it was amazing. The stage was getting ripped apart, the wind was blowing so hard, and I felt like that guitar guy in *Mad Max: Fury Road*. By the end of the show, kids with hypothermia were being carted off, and the festival got shut down because of the electrical risk. But man, I was just like, "That fucking ROCKED!"

There was the incident where Slipknot watched me knock myself unconscious. I can't remember where it was, which isn't surprising, but it was some festival where we shared a bill with Slipknot. When you're playing and the stage lights hit, they tighten up your pupils. When it's dark and you walk off stage, you're basically blind, and that's why there's always a guy with a flashlight. The last thing I remember was talking to Slipknot, who were watching from the side of the stage. That was strange enough because I was thinking, "Why the fuck is Slipknot into Third Eye Blind?" I shook their hands, said, "Nice to meet you guys," then I stepped right off the stage into a black hole. I caught myself on the chin and knocked myself out. They had to haul me out on a stretcher, and I was so fucking embarrassed.

Our big break gig is still so vivid to me. It was right before our record deal, and I met with David Massey, who was an A&R guy at Epic Records in New York. His big artist was Oasis, and this was back when A&R people really had power. I can't stand it when someone has power over me. It's my punk rock roots, and I can't abide authority. We just need to fuck with them, otherwise we wouldn't be artists. We'd just be song-and-dance people or *American Idol* finalists. Suddenly, all these labels and A&R people were looking at us, and I felt like a lap dancer.

I was sitting in Massey's office, and he has an elegant, officiant British accent. He was dribbling, but not shooting baskets, which is what had been happening with everyone I had met. I interrupted and said, "So, what can I do for you?" It was pretty rude, but I couldn't talk small talk for one more fucking second. He said, "Well, you can sign to Epic Records." Finally, someone had offered us a deal. He asked when he could see us next, and I happened to know that Oasis was playing the Civic Center a few days later in San Francisco. I told him we'd like to open the show. He studied me for a second as he was beginning to realize who he was dealing with—someone who had the audacity to ask for something like that.

He picked up the phone and called Oasis's tour manager. In his very British accent, he says, "Hello James! How are ya, mate? I've got a band here who would like to open for Oasis. Do you have an open spot?" Massey said to me, "OK, you're in." My immediate response was panic. Shit, we had only played in front of fifty-five people. This was the Civic Center, which held about 8,000. Keep in mind, this was the peak of Oasis mania as well. We had only played for really small audiences at the Paradise Lounge. Even then, I played the Paradise Lounge like it was Wembley Stadium—playing all the way to the back of the room. My thinking was always to not play the room you're in but the biggest room in your mind.

Before we went on stage, we were all shaking like greyhounds. I said to the guys, "We're gonna bury Oasis. We are gonna destroy and fuck them up. When we're done, everyone is going to leave because we were the main event. Everyone walk out on stage like you are the baddest motherfuckers who have ever walked on a stage." I said all of that but didn't believe any of it. I don't know what we sounded like that night, but afterwards they tripled our pay. Sherry Wasserman, who was the promoter, has been a friend and mentor to me ever since. They pushed us back out for an encore, which blew us away because opening bands never get encores.

The next day, the headline was "Unknown local band upstages Oasis." We didn't upstage them, but they were really lackluster that night. After our set, we went backstage and Noel Gallagher was looking bored. Liam said, "You were shite, mate." I said, "Dude, we blew you out. We just buried you." He respected that because they come from that British pub culture where they're always testing each other. That was the first moment where I thought that maybe we could do this.

Live performance is a really important part of my life, and maybe the most important. I've always wondered why, and this is the conclusion I've come to: It's not about bearing witness to a DJ while he stands over his computer. A lot of bands are Mac-Book Pro rock, where they're playing along to a sequencer. A show can either fly or fall apart based on the actions and empathy of the musicians playing, and if all goes right, the musicians are conjured up out of themselves. You start feeling things, and that's what music is about. That collective, emotional moment let's people know that they are not alone. We're all connected on a very deep level, through fury, folly, lust, and whimsy. I feel a glorious connection, and it's worth every smashed chin and fucked up gig.

43

BUZZ OSBORNE

(Melvins)

Osborne throws more shade than hip-hop artists, and we love him for it. Here, he calls out Rob Zombie, the Ozzfest staff, and recounts the time a young, female fan attempted suicide on his stage. Memo to bands that open for Buzz: Don't piss him off.

There was a time in the '90s when we were opening for a lot of bands, which basically means you're trying to sell your band to an audience that isn't your own. We didn't really care that much about that. We did whole tours that were just horrendous, and that wasn't only coming from the audience. We did a tour with White Zombie that was easily the worst touring experience of my entire life. Everything about it sucked from top to bottom. The crew were a bunch of fucking assholes, and the crowds didn't care about us. I can deal with the crowd, but Rob Zombie himself was a fucking dick. I don't know how else to put it. And there was absolutely no reason for it either. I've been around guys I consider *real* rock stars. Gene Simmons and Paul Stanley never treated me like that. Those guys are totally cool! They go out of their way to say hello to me. They're not acting like prima donna dickheads. So why the fuck would Zombie do it? It makes me hate these lower-level, lower-echelon fuckheads even more. They're pissing on my lawn. If I had to do that tour over again, I would walk the first day.

Let me tell you about the Ozzfest people! Total fucking assholes. They couldn't have cared less about us. We got on that tour because Tool said they wanted one band on the bill that they liked or they wouldn't do it. We agreed, and even with Tool backing us, the Ozzfest people were like, "We don't care about the Melvins." They made sure that we understood that every step of the way. Ozzy doesn't know his birthday, so he didn't know what was going on. It's not like he told everyone to be dicks to us. When you see Ozzy sitting in the kitchen coloring like a five-year-old kid, that should tell you where his head's at. Does that mean I'm not a fan of Ozzy or Sabbath? Not at all! Ozzy has bigger problems putting two plus two together than worrying about us. But the powers that be, the top brass of that organization, went out of their way to be total fucking assholes.

It was just like the top brass of the White Zombie people. The manager was OK and was nice to me. But the rest of them went out of their way to be complete assholes for no reason other than to make us miserable. The sound guy came up to us on the first day and said, "I am going to see to it that you never sound as good as White Zombie." He just told us that to our faces, and guess what? He wasn't lying. That's exactly what he did. He was a fucking pain in the ass the entire tour. That's why I *hate* that shit! I fucking hate big wheel tours like that.

I never act like that to people, and there's a reason why. I am not going to be that guy. It takes more effort to be a fucking asshole than it does to be nice. There's just no excuse for it. Aside from their shitty music that I'm not into anyway, I don't have any interest in it. If I'm going to a hockey arena, I want to see hockey, not a show. If you're a sixteen-year-old kid on acid and you're just away from your parents for the night. That's fine. I get it! I'm not saying everyone shouldn't experience that. It's just not for me and what drove me to the intimate settings of punk rock as a teenager. That spoke to me more—in a way that seemed more human than an arena.

Believe me, I've moved on in my life. I've put my money where my mouth is. I do eighty to one hundred and twenty shows a year and have every year for the last thirty years. I've put out at least one album a year, and I've done that since the '80s. It's not like I'm just sitting around bitching and complaining. I do my job, and these are just my observations. If people want to think I'm just jealous of Ozzy or Zombie, it doesn't help me to complain about them. If I wanted to help myself, I'd act like these people are amazing and they were great and totally cool with me. I'm not jealous of their fame. If I have to be Ozzy Osbourne to attain that level of fame, I'll happily stay right where I'm at. I don't want to be Rob Zombie! I have zero interest.

My story has not changed one iota over the years. It's just the facts, and I'm like an elephant. I don't forget, and my truth is not elastic. Hate me...good! The most offensive thing about me is how our music sounds. But I'm offended by horrible music all the time. Since I was twelve-years-old, I think most music is terrible. There's a few glimmers that fall through the cracks that raise my hope. You have to understand that I'm a music fan like you wouldn't believe. No art form ever has moved me the way music has in my life. I talked to a guy once who was an Indy car driver in the early '70s. He told me that the only other thing that turned him on, apart from driving an Indy car at top speed, was music. That's how powerful it is.

Nothing will put a fucking charge up my ass like music. Nothing ever has. It's what makes me got out of bed and tie my shoes. So when things like Ozzfest or Zombie happen, I am deeply offended because I feel so strongly about the power of music. It offends me so much that I'll never be able to walk away from it. They are defiling the church. They are cheapening the art and bringing it down to a level where I just want their fucking heads on a stake. If this wasn't a civilized world, all their heads would be on stakes.

We played a show with Mr. Bungle in the early '90s, and this was after Mike Patton was the MTV poster boy with Faith No More. As a result, his other band, Mr. Bungle, also got signed to Warner Bros. Mr. Bungle is a much different band than Faith No More, and they certainly don't write bright and breezy pop tunes. They're much weirder, and Mike would do most of those sets wearing a mask. A lot of times people didn't even know which guy he was. The MTV crowd—or as we called them, the "baby rockers"— had no interest in the Melvins at all. It was a vicious nightmare of people hating our guts.

Those baby rockers gave us so much shit at one show that backstage, Patton was pissed. Keep in mind, Mr. Bungle had hand selected us to play with them. The audiences never seemed to put it together that we were a band that the headliners liked. I take great offense to that, and I would be pissed if that ever happened to a band opening for us. It's just totally disrespectful. So, Patton is pissed. He's fuming, "That was fucked up! I can't believe this." He tore up his setlist and said that he was changing it specially for tonight. He wrote out several lists, handed it to his band members, and all it said was, "Tonight, they will pay."

They go out and do a total white-noise, nightmarish set that included Patton sticking an eyedropper up his ass, giving the crowd an enema. Most people missed it, but trust me, he did it. He did it more than once at shows. Now it would be on YouTube, but you could get away with it back then. You'd probably be brought up on charges today. The craziest thing I've ever seen on tour was with Patton's band Fantomas somewhere in France. It was me, Patton, Trevor Dunn from Mr. Bungle, and Dave Lombardo from Slayer on drums. We were playing a festival and halfway through the set, a girl climbed the lighting rig. She wrapped the mic cable around her neck and tried to hang herself onstage.

She was hanging by her fucking neck, and her weight dropped the rig low enough that someone was able to raise her up and cut the fucking cord. That's what the French do! We got backstage and she's sitting in our fucking dressing room. I yell, "What the fuck is this?" We called security and explained that she just tried to kill herself. She's like, "What's wrong?" I go, "Where we come from, it's not OK to kill yourself!" That girl needed serious help, and I was not the one to give it to her. She's mumbling in this thick French accent, "Yes, maybe you're right." Goddamn I'm right! Some of the people were saying, "Yeah, she was acting weird all day." Really, ya think?

We opened for Nine Inch Nails where people were literally ripping up the floorboards. It was another goddamn hockey arena, and they were ripping the wood covering off the ground, setting it on fire, and throwing it at us. We didn't stop playing. NIN were going to shoot a concert movie that night, and the audience was obviously going fucking berserk while we were playing. I was thinking how crazy the place was going to go when Trent [Reznor] came out. He walked out at the end of our set and said, "That's fucking it! I don't want to see anybody throwing any more shit, or we're not gonna play." All the energy got sucked out of the place. They filmed, the show was totally lackluster, and they shit-canned the whole thing. We drove all the hate and adrenaline out of the crowd. This was the height of the *Downward Spiral* era, so Trent was God. Those guys were totally nice to us and no problems behind the scenes. Everyone there was totally cool. But anyway, I'm one happy son of a bitch, and I love what I do.

44

CHOPMASTER J

(Digital Underground)

Apart from the "Humpty Dance," Digital Underground was also famous for introducing the world to a young Tupac Shakur, who came into the group as a roadie. You'll love the story about Pac's fake gold chain.

Dig this. The 1990 Houston Summit jumbotron incident with Public Enemy on the Fear of a Black Planet Tour. The stage guys warn you about what to do and what not to do when you hit the stage. It was my first time being onstage in an arena with a jumbotron. They tell you not to watch yourself on the jumbotron because you'll fuck up and trip or something. I'm like, "Shit, OK, OK." We're onstage, I'm rocking, and we're doing "Doowutchyalike" from the Underground record *Sex Packets*. When the chorus comes in on that song, I would jump off my riser where I was doing my samples and percussion. I jump down and grab the champagne, which I start masturbating into the crowd. I'm also throwing popcorn and confetti, yelling, "Do What Cha Like! Do What Cha Like" and running around this big-ass stage.

I look up at the jumbotron, thinking, "Oh wow, this is really incredible!" For the second verse, I went back to my position on the riser doing my thing. Then the chorus comes back, and I jump off again. This time, I'm watching myself run on the jumbotron. Problem is, when you're watching yourself on that thing, you're not watching the stage. I flew right off the motherfucking stage with a bucket of popcorn in my arms. It was so embarrassing. I fell off because I got caught up in my own vanity and hype. Guilty as charged. I landed down in the pit. You would have thought the crowd would have caught me, but that shit opened up like I was Moses, and I just went splat, right on my back off an arena-size stage. That shit hurt, man!

I sprung back up and scrambled onstage like it didn't hurt. All my bandmates were cracking up, and they couldn't even do the chorus. It was probably the most humiliating moment in my career. No one ever let me get over that. Do you know what it's like to get teased by Flavor Flav? You don't wanna know. Tupac was there for that too.

One time, we were on the Big Daddy Kane tour in the spring of 1990 with Pac. He was only eighteen and wasn't a rapper yet. He was more of a sound guy and stage manager at the time. It was the first time that we gave him a mic, basically so he could be a backup MC. During the "Humpty Dance" he'd co-sign on shit, like yelling "Humpty!" and "Wave your hands in the air!" He held the mic down into the monitor, which he didn't know creates a feedback response. He kept doing that, and he was swearing up and down that the sound guy was trying to sabotage him. That's what Pac would do—he'd get all agitated and start making shit up in his head. He'd swear by it, then want to fight about it. He would never take the blame for anything. His response was to attack. I'd really have to check him hard and make him accountable to help him pick his fights. He was lovable, but he was wild.

He was eighteen and had just left the projects. He was on an arena tour with some of the biggest acts in hip-hop. He believed in provoking then befriending you. For example, we were at the Joe Louis arena in Detroit in 1990. If you look up into the rafters to the side of the stage, there's always people hanging out. Pac looks up, and there's some Detroit locals razzing him about his jewelry being fake because he used to wear all these chains and stuff. Pac gets into a shouting match with these dudes hanging in the wings. He's yelling crazy shit, and they're yelling, "Punk ass, that's why your jewelry is fake!" Pac was getting so heated that he gets into it with us. He's like, "Those motherfuckers are yelling shit! If you don't help me, y'all ain't shit!"

I said to him calmly, "But Pac, that shit around your neck *is* fake." He wasn't *Tupac* yet; he was roadie Tupac at that point. He's still going crazy, and it's like, why get into a shouting match with the audience that paid to come see us? It didn't make sense. What, you gonna beat somebody up that called your fake jewelry fake? If I hadn't talked him down, he would have hunted those dudes down after the show. He was the guy that would challenge the old, white waitress at the Waffle House in Oklahoma about his fork being dirty. It's three in the morning and Pac's accusing her of being racist and giving him a dirty fork.

That's the kinda shit when I'd tell him, "Man, you gonna get us killed." It was 1990 and we were in Oklahoma. You couldn't do that shit. The police were protesting our tour because they had confused Public Enemy with N.W.A. and thought they were the ones that did "Fuck tha Police." The white folks in Oklahoma didn't give a shit. They just didn't like us anyway. Pac was always putting us in precarious positions like that. Flav was kinda like that too. I don't know if he got really into crack a bit later—like when crack would fall out of his pocket onstage. But he was smoking during our time with him, and sometimes he would stay in the town that we had just left. If we were in Phoenix, he would have been hooked up with some chick doing his thing, and we'd just leave him.

Sometimes Public Enemy wouldn't even know he was gone. Chuck would hit the stage, and when they'd yell for Flav to come out, he wasn't there. The whole thing was they'd come onstage at different times and then yell for the other to come out. There were a few nights where it was just Chuck out there, because Flav was late or stuck in some other city. Flav was a wild dude, but he also plays classical piano and speaks four different languages. Anyway, I'm about to go to sleep now. I ate a bunch of them edible Tootsie Roll things with the THC in them.

45

KENNY LOGGINS

Kenny has always been one of those guys I wondered about in their '80s period—meaning was he completely blown out on cocaine? Turns out, just a little. He also talks about poor fashion choices and a disastrous opening slot for Curtis Mayfield.

Thank you for making me dredge up these memories, many of which I've successfully repressed. The first story that comes to mind was back when I was in college. I got an offer to go on tour with a rock band called the Electric Prunes. My friend Jeremy Stuart was the music director and keyboardist, so he brought me in as a singing guitar player. At that point, I'd already written "Danny's Song" and "House at Pooh Corner." Those were the songs that always worked for me, and Jeremy figured he'd restructure the Electric Prunes show to do a break in the middle for my songs. The Prunes were a psychedelic rock act from the mid- to late '60s. I was definitely not a psychedelic rock person, although I did like some of it.

I was more of an acoustic guy, like Dylan, Donovan, and Tim Hardin. Those were my idols at the time. So, I hit the road with the Prunes, and I had never been on a tour before. I was only eighteen and pretty nervous. We instituted that break in the show, where I would sing "Danny's Song" and "House at Pooh Corner." Up to that point, I had never experienced what it was like to truly fail or bomb on stage. People were walking out of the show during my songs because they weren't there for that. They wanted a trippy, psychedelic experience, and here I was doing these quiet, acoustic songs. It was a very important lesson for me to learn, albeit very difficult.

When Loggins and Messina started up when I was twenty-two, I would wake up with cold sweats during the night, reliving those Electric Prunes failures. It was truly traumatic for me, and I was developing a bit of stage fright. I learned that I had to be smart about my audience. When I was in high school, I would enter talent shows, but I never won. One time I lost to a guy who imitated Bob Dylan. Then I lost to a group of high school girls in black light hula skirts who did a hula dance, and the judges went wild. A black light dance was the height of entertainment in the 1960s. Let's just say I had a very rocky entrance into show business. I never took into account the "show" aspect of show business. Presentation matters!

I began to realize that things like wardrobe mattered, but Messina and I had as much wardrobe as the Eagles. It wasn't much, but we would wear the local football or hockey jerseys of the touring cities. That was about as snazzy as we got, and you can see us on the cover of *Rolling Stone* with shirts that are way too tight and pants that are too short. You might say I've been wardrobe challenged my entire career. I did a lot of research on lighting and sound companies, so I was a lot better at the visual and aural presentation.

Fashion is a weird thing, and my biggest offense was the *Keep the Fire* album cover. It was based on a Halloween costume I'd had previous to that shoot. I enjoyed the idea of playing Gandalf, and that was really where I was going with that fashion choice. I don't think the photography quite captured what I was going for. I've taken a lot of teasing for that cover, but lately, my younger audience thinks that it's really cool. They say beauty is in the eye of the beholder, and I've had a number of fashion faux pas that I've committed over the years. It really all adds up to nothing in the long run.

When Loggins and Messina first went out on the road, it was as an opening act for Delaney & Bonnie and Billy Preston. We did a winter tour, and back east somewhere there was a blizzard. The promotor hadn't put up the deposit, so none of us were going on. Our road managers were huddled in the back room with the promotors, and some kids who were waiting for the show threw rocks through the dressing room window. We panicked and thought there was going to be a riot. I said to Messina, "I think they're going to fucking rip us to shreds," so we ran onstage and started playing. That settled everyone down, but I had never seen an audience so hostile.

One time in Boston years ago with Messina, it was raining like crazy, and the promoter was fighting with our road manager about whether it was safe to play. We thought it was too wet and too dangerous to go on stage, but the promoter kept insisting it wasn't. He went on stage to announce that the show was happening rain or shine and that the audience shouldn't be afraid of a little rain. At that exact moment, he got struck by lightning and had to be transported to the hospital. It was really a bad day for that guy. The kicker was that it didn't rain enough to the point where he could collect insurance. He was majorly fucked. I've butted heads with a lot of promoters over the years, but the only artist I've never gotten along with is Glenn Frey. There's a lot of horror stories about those boys, but Glenn tops my list. It's too soon since his passing to get really into it, but someday somebody should write a book about the guy. He was just a really unhappy guy.

One of my most embarrassing moments was with Loggins and Messina when we played the Troubadour in LA, opening for Curtis Mayfield. It was a ridiculous double-bill, but Clive Davis made it happen. In those days, we would start the shows with me going on stage alone to do "Danny's Song" and some acoustic stuff. Then Jimmy [Messina] would come out with the band. I was doing the opening solo thing at the Troubadour, and the audience was 90 percent black. There were two really beautiful black women in the front row because at the Troubadour in those days, the audience would sit right in front of the stage. I was singing my songs, and they were looking at me, yelling "Get down! Get down!"

I thought I was doing really good and that they were yelling it like, "Get down! Get funky!" I just thought it was the best gig ever and that I had completely won over the crowd. Finally, Jimmy comes on stage and whispered, "Man, I don't know how you did that. Those girls were telling you to get down off the stage the whole time." My face turned bright red, and I could barely look at the audience for the rest of the set.

I had a short dance with cocaine in the '80s, but it was not my drug and didn't last very long. Thankfully, I didn't lose my brain or my voice to drugs or alcohol. I've never smoked cigarettes, but I did smoke marijuana in the early days. I found that it was difficult to perform high because I kept forgetting where I was in the song. I would mix up the verses, and then I'd get really paranoid so I stopped doing that. As for the paranoia thing, I never knew when I'd slip from having a great time on stage to thinking someone in the crowd was heckling me, to the point where "Get down" becomes "No. Get down!"

I still love playing for a real audience that has paid good money to see me. It's more difficult with the corporate audiences. They didn't buy a ticket and, quite often, they don't even know who they're going to see that night. The company president made the decision because he or she is a fan. It's usually a good audience but not great. Usually, they yell, "Danger Zone" at me. It used to be "Footloose," but because of the show *Archer* and a few other high-profile things, it's usually "Danger Zone." Truthfully, while I do not always want to play them, I'm lucky and glad that those songs have lasted all these years.

46

BRENT SMITH

(Shinedown)

Hard-rock outfit Shinedown was fairly new to me before this book, but I'm glad I spoke with front man Smith, who shared one of my very favorite stories. Take note: If you ever find yourself backstage at a show next to a deli tray, try giving someone a "smoking gun."

One story that immediately comes to mind was from the very beginning of our career, from the very humble beginnings of Shinedown. This was from late 2003 or early 2004, when we got a huge opportunity to open for Van Halen. They had reunited with Sammy Hagar. It was a two-month tour in really big markets, and every show was sold out. Our first album came out in 2003, and we had only been playing 200–500 capacity clubs before that. When we got on tour, with me being full of testosterone, I was gonna make everybody in the building pay attention. We only had about thirty-five minutes, and with only seven songs in the set, I really tried to make my performance count.

I began to notice that a kid was in the VIP pit every night, watching intently. Those seats were insanely expensive, and sometimes he was the only one in there. About eight shows into the tour, the kid came into the dressing room. It was Wolfgang Van Halen, Eddie's son. He was only about eleven at the time and was out on the road with his dad. He really liked us, and Eddie started showing up in the pit to watch us with Wolfie. That allowed me to befriend Eddie on the tour, and we got to be buds. He just started hanging around. He flew private jets everywhere and would show up around 5:00 p.m. every day and pop his head in the dressing room.

We'd go to catering together. I noticed that he just wanted somebody to talk to and that he seemed kind of lonely. I think he liked that I wasn't some fanatic Van Halen fan, as I only really knew their singles growing up. I didn't see any in-fighting between Eddie and the band, but I never did see them together offstage. Alex and Eddie were always kind of around each other, and Sammy and Michael kind of shadowed each other, but I never saw them all together.

Eddie had just gotten his second hip replacement, and he had just beaten cancer. He was drinking though, and I say with all sincerity that he was a really wonderful, endearing soul, but here's where the story comes in. Eddie rolled into my dressing room while I was in the bathroom taking a piss. I washed my hands, but didn't dry them all the way. I was patting them on my jeans, and I gave Eddie a handshake/hi-five thing. He yelled, "Motherfucker, you got piss on your hands?" I said jokingly, "No man, I just had to rub one out in the bathroom." He looked at me sideways, walked over to our craft service table, and proceeded to urinate on the deli meat tray.

He was smoking a cigarette, and he rolled up the lit cigarette in a pissy slice of turkey. He handed me the deli tray and said, "Give this to your tour manager. It's called a smoking gun." Then he walked out of the room like nothing had happened. He will never fucking remember this story if he reads this book, I guarantee it. I wasn't offended, mad, or disgusted by what he had done. It was such a rock 'n' roll moment that I had electricity running through me. There was no malice in his actions, and it felt like one of the folkloric rock stories you hear about that aren't true. That shit doesn't happen, right? I'm here to say yes...it does.

Here's a funny one from the first time Shinedown played the Download Festival in the UK. We were on the second stage in front of about 80,000 people, and they had these humongous jumbo-trons on both sides of the stage. When I say they were huge, I mean they were freaking gigantic. We're going hard, and at the end of our set, our bassist Eric Bass had a wardrobe malfunction. He was wearing all white for whatever reason at the time. He had these white jeans that he had been wearing for about a year on tour, and he kept talking about the jeans not having many more jumps and splits left in them. I kept telling him to put on some fucking new pants, but he liked the way they were broken in.

We're up there doing our thing, and Eric's jumping around and doing splits like the madman he is. After the last song, he's holding the bass up in the air, and all these girls are totally wide-eyed. It was a weird reaction, and we realized that Eric had split his pants in the front. Usually you split your pants in the back, but his gave out in the front. He was going commando like he always does, and his junk was hanging out the front of his pants for all of the UK to see on the jumbotron. At that moment, he was literally the biggest dick in the UK.

He just had to own it. They say TV adds ten pounds? Those screens added 150. He had so much adrenaline going that he didn't notice it. It might have felt a little windy down there, but he just kept holding that bass in the air. We were walking off stage, and he was kinda shuffling funny because those pants were split wide open. He looked down and looked up with these wild eyes. He played it totally cool and just had to laugh it off. Thank God he had to retire those pants.

47

GARY LEVOX

(Rascal Flatts)

I'm not a country music guy by any stretch, but I definitely didn't want to alienate any genre based on personal taste. I'm not sure if LeVox was afraid to tell me any truly gnarly stories, but with sixteen number one songs, I honestly believe that they just didn't have time to get truly out of control.

This one is really weird, and it's a miracle I didn't get seriously hurt. It was the beginning of our tour a few years back, so the set and everything was new. A few weeks in, I told my stage manager, "Dude, I can't see where I'm walking out there." Usually there's glow-in-the-dark tape to mark the edges and outline of the stage. When the spotlights went dark, it was totally black for me, and I couldn't see squat. I was getting worried I would torpedo right off the stage, and it was about a ten foot drop to the ground. Sure enough, one night I was singing, and brother—I just walked straight off the stage. The weird thing was everything went quiet, and it was like I went deaf for about five seconds. I landed square on my feet, right in the middle of the audience. I didn't really know what had happened, and I just stood there.

All the camera phones came out, and it was like an out-of-body experience. It was almost like I had floated down there. The baseball player Johnny Damon was there, and we hung out with him after the show. He gave me a baseball that read, "To Gary, nice recovery bro." Another bad one was when we were playing an outdoor festival with a huge, elevated stage. The camera guys were shooting up at us, and putting it up on the jumbotron. It was our second song, and the crotch completely ripped out of my pants. As it was only the second song, I'm thinking, "Dammit—what am I gonna do for the next hour?" I jumped up on the drum riser and yelled at our drummer Jim Riley, "Did my pants just rip?" He's banging away and yells back, "Yep," with a big smile on his face. I had to reach down and wrangle one of the camera guys. "Dude, please don't shoot me from that angle!" I had to sing with my feet together for the whole show.

When you go from being an opening act and take that lead to headliner, it's either gonna work or it's not, and it's scary. The people suddenly weren't buying tickets to Kenny Chesney or Brooks & Dunn with us included. It was suddenly all on us, and I wasn't sure if I was ready. It was a really scary time in my career because the last thing you want to do is fail at something you love. Thankfully, that self-doubt went away because I knew we were ready. We started with Jo Dee Messina, Toby Keith, Brooks & Dunn and finally Kenny Chesney. We were building up hits, but even with four singles, that's only thirteen minutes of music. What were we gonna do with the other forty-five minutes? Our plan was to build it up as big as possible before going out on our own.

We've had people turn on us and been heckled a bunch of times. Early on, it was mostly girls coming out to the shows. There'd be a ton of high school girls who had dragged their boyfriends along. They'd come back for the meet-n-greet and would literally say, "I don't even want to be here, but she made me come." This one time in Colorado, there was a whole wrestling team at the show that was throwing rocks at us. They hit our fiddle player and drummer and banged up our instruments. Finally, the wrestling coach realized what was going out and threw them out. A few years ago, we were opening for the Rolling Stones at the Indy 500. Stones fans are so incredibly passionate and don't want to sit through an opening act. They were flipping us off and heckling the entire show. I was thinking, "This is crazy! These senior citizens are flipping me the bird!" There was a woman who had to be at least seventy-eight, flipping me off and flashing me. You don't forget that kinda thing.

Nowadays, somebody gets two hits and they're out there headlining. You can only play "Sweet Home Alabama" so many times in a forty-five-minute set. You gotta be ready for that main stage. Our first single went number one, and it really hasn't stopped. It's been eighteen years and sixteen number one songs. Twenty-six million records sold. It really has been a whirlwind. We were in our early twenties and didn't really know how to take it. I was the only one that was married. It was as crazy as you can imagine, with no sleep. We were working so hard, doing three radio stations a day. We were touring and cutting records while on tour, and it's been that way for the past fifteen years. Last year, we only did thirty-five shows, and that was us essentially taking the year off.

Because of that crazy schedule, you'll never see us on *Behind the Music: The Drug Years*. There just really wasn't time. We were doing stuff that no one had done before. We were the first country act to play and sell out Wrigley Field and the first country band to do three sold-out shows at Madison Square Garden. We were high on our career. The best training ground for me was the early days, playing bars and honky-tonks in Nashville. I learned what worked on stage and how to talk to the crowd. I really honed my craft in those whiskey joints. With *American Idol* or *The Voice*, you've got winners who have never even sang in a club with no training on how to be a front man or woman.

Man, people love to fight in those honky-tonks. People get hammered and just lose their minds, and I've had to get physical a bunch of times. They're trying to test you. The bars don't close until 3:00 a.m. in Nashville, so we were up there from 9:00 p.m.– 3:00 a.m. By the time we'd get outside, people were going to work. It was like, "What the hell are we doing? What kind of life are we living?" I had a bunch of moments when I thought about quitting, especially before we got our record deal. I'm originally from Ohio, and I had a state job for ten years. I left a good job with benefits to chase this dream and starve. I don't know how many times I called my mom, freaking out that I couldn't do it.

When we first started, we were working off of tips only. One night, Jay [DeMarcus] had his keyboard set up on the floor by a cigarette machine. I was sitting on a stool, and that was our set-up for the night. We made twenty-seven cents one night, and that's a true story. I looked at Jay and said, "How the hell are we going to split this?" Touring has gotten better with age for me because I appreciate it so much more. Country fans are loyal to the end, and I believe they're the most loyal in the music business. With pop, hip-hop, or rock, I don't think their fans are any less passionate— I'm just not sure that they'll stay with a band for as long as country fans. We have four generations of fans coming out to our shows, from grandmothers to granddaughters. We had a lady schedule her C-section around our tour date. That's fan loyalty, man.

48

STEWART COPELAND

(the Police)

I'm one of those people that finds Sting funny on general principle, so it was a total delight to hear Copeland yell expletives into the phone, describing one of the many battles he waged with the Tantric God.

We were total straight arrows when it came to playing shows. I discovered at an early age that playing drunk or on drugs just didn't work, but it wasn't for lack of trying. The worst thing that can happen to a drummer happened to me at Madison Square Garden. It was our first arena show, and it was a huge deal for us. We had worked our way up from small clubs to big clubs, from theaters to big theaters. The jump from the biggest theater—around three or four thousand—to the smallest arena of eighteen thousand is a very big jump. Shit, I was nervous. Along with worrying about selling enough tickets, it's a whole different audio environment.

A few songs into our set, we were thinking, "This is really cold. The audience is so far away." The Madison Square Garden stage is very high compared to a theater or club. It was lonely up there—just three guys in a very big room. Then the worst thing I could have imagined happened: The skin of my bass drum cracked. If you lose a snare drum, you pull it and put in another without missing a beat. Same thing with a tom-tom or really anything else in a drum kit. If something goes wrong with a guitar, it's no problem. There's always one waiting to switch out. With a kick drum, you have to stop the show, pull out all the mic stands and the cymbals and drums. Getting to the very bottom of the drum set is hell on earth.

So the show stopped, and our whole crew swarmed the stage. They were tearing apart this jungle, trying to get to the bottom of that damn kick drum. I'm sweating, just waiting out the whole thing. Fortunately, our singer, front man, and star, had a couple tricks up his sleeve. Sting started doing running commentary: "Hey! Here comes Dave, and he's got the cymbal! Oh, he dropped it!" He sounded like a carnival barker, that Sting-O. He had learned patter and how to bullshit an audience from our early club days. He's cracking jokes, singing "The Yellow Rose of Texas" and whatever he could think of to keep the show going. "They got the skin! They've got the drum back on the stand! They've got the mic and the cymbals back! OK, are you ready to rock!" All of Madison Square Garden, in fact, all of Manhattan, belonged to us after that. When you make a mistake and there's an epic car crash onstage, that's what the audience remembers. That's my advice to all young musicians.

I don't think most audiences were aware, but we had temper tantrums onstage all the time. We were playing an ancient stadium in Turin, Italy, that had since been turned into a football stadium. The stage was down at one end of the stadium, and the dressing rooms for the players and us were in the middle, at the center line. To get from the dressing rooms to behind the stage, we had to take these little mini-buses. There were 80,000 people in the crumbling stadium, waiting to see us. It was Sting's birthday, and I gave him a tuba. Three happy, blond heads got into the minibus, ready to play a show. The bus started taking all these weird turns, and the next thing we knew, we found ourselves merging onto a freeway outside the stadium. I yelled, "What the fuck?"

The giant stadium, which blocked out the sky, was suddenly in our rearview mirror. We had a police entourage with blasting sirens, escorting us away from our gig, heading God knows where. After some yelling, we took the next off-ramp and got back on track, but now it was rush hour. We must have looked ridiculous in that minibus. We had our headsets on—I had my headband going—with nowhere to go. We circled the entrance a couple times because the drivers didn't know the proper entrance. We were essentially lost in the parking lot. We got on stage about thirty minutes late, but that was all preamble for the meltdown that was to come.

For some reason, halfway through the first song, our illustrious, esteemed lead singer was not happy. I knew what it was. It was because I sped up that second verse going into the chorus. I just loved that chorus, but we were playing it twice the normal speed. Our singer was not happy, to say the least. He was looking back at me, hurling daggers and trying to show me where the back-beat was. Generally, that's not something that cheers me up. I don't like having the guy at the front of the stage, indicating the timing with his left hand, which should have been thumping his fucking bass. "You miserable, cocksucking, motherfucking, piece of shit, bitch, goddammit *I'll fucking kill you!*" In front of 80,000 people.

I had white-hot popping balloons for eyes I was so pissed. I was smacking those cymbals so fucking hard they were standing vertically. You can only hit a drum so hard before it clacks instead of thumps, so that was an exciting evening. Once again, the audience loves that shit! We would take that anger backstage too. So many nights we'd be screaming at each other unintelligibly. Since both of us lack emotional stamina, we'd desperately be trying to sustain this towering, glorious rage, but it would dissipate. It would end up being, "Aww fuck. You prick...c'mere!" Much to Andy Summers's [guitarist] confusion and disappointment, we'd be back to hugging and kissing each other.

It never came to blows between Sting and I, but there were a couple tussles. But during those tussles, we'd be laughing hysterically, so I don't think that counts. There was an accidental broken rib at Shea Stadium though. All the British press and tabloids were there, signifying that another British band had conquered America. We were there, the three blonde heads, goofing around like The Monkees for the cameras. Sting grabbed my copy of *The New York Times* I was reading, by way of frolic, but I reacted with, "Hey, fuck you!" Immediately, these two young twenty-somethings were fighting it out over a newspaper, with all the cameras on us. During the course of this, I had an elbow, he had a rib, and the two reached unity.

I had an uncomfortable sensation elbowing him, and the next thing I knew, Sting had a fractured rib. I mumbled, "Ahh shit. Sorry dude." We still played the show that night, and Sting killed it! It turned out to be a little hairline fracture, but I know he was still in pain. That's the true story, and don't believe the legend that I broke his rib in some crazy brawl.

49

DAN AYKROYD

(Blues Brothers)

This chapter was bizarre from the start, as I never actually got a chance to correspond directly with Aykroyd. Even his manager was surprised that he wanted to contribute, and a few weeks later, I got a short story written by Aykroyd. He misunderstood or just didn't want to share stories about the Blues Brothers. I like the way it's written, so I hope you'll enjoy it as well, even if there's no dirt on Belushi. Sorry!

Please find below my written account for your use as you see fit of the worst rock 'n' roll concert I ever attended. On March 2, 1967 Eric Burdon and The Animals were booked to play the Coliseum, a 5,000-seater in my hometown of Ottawa, Ontario Canada. The group was at their peak with the hits "House of the Rising Sun," "We Gotta Get Out of This Place," "Help Me Girl," etc. At the time, I was on the cusp of mid-teenhood, attending St. Pius the Tenth Minor Preparatory Seminary for Boys. A few of my dormmates and I pooled our altar boy service fees to buy tickets for the show.

It was a windblown end of winter night as ten of us put on our jean jackets and Half-Wellington boots to conform with the look of every other male who would be there. Joining us were our handful of lady friends from the local mall in beehive hair, pegged jeans, and black Converse sneakers or boots. We were all set with flasks of rye and mixed vodka anticipating the coming onslaught of this dynamic English band's powerful and, for us at that age, very evocative music. After a tremendous organ-driven set by Question Mark and the Mysterians ("96 Tears"), we awaited the feature artists, and we awaited and awaited and awaited—a half hour, then an hour going into an hour and a half. We began to chant: "We want The Animals! We want Eric!" At this point a muted strain of conversation began to ripple through the crowd: "They aren't going on! The promoter bolted with the money! He didn't pay the band!"

As half the house now registered this information, multiple clusters of concert-goers began to smash chairs on the floor, storm the stage, and destroy benches in the stands. My friends and I were swept up in these frenzied waves of protest at the grave injustices being perpetrated: Our idols were being robbed, we wouldn't get to see them play, and the promoter had already left the building. My own personal hand in the destructive riot was assisting in the dismantling of a couple of telephone booths. When someone—not me—threw a lit, fluid-coated, flaming Zippo onto the torn pages of the Ottawa phone book, our contingent exited the building just as squads of city police began to arrive.

Upon returning back to the dorm at St. Pius, we were more adrenalin-fueled, exhilarated, and indeed happier than if we actually had heard The Animals play. 2000 teens became animals

instead. Moreover, the night was a perfect outlet for us young sem-
inarians after a long winter. Plus, the Coliseum needed a complete
renovation anyway.

ROBERT POLLARD

(Guided By Voices)

Best known for power pop anthems, high-kicks, a lo-fi aesthetic, and seri-ously heroic drinking, GBV broke out during the indie rock explosion of the early '90s. Notoriously interview-shy, Pollard wrote his own chap-ter, revealing that New York hipsters are far more terrifying than aggro metalheads.

Written by Robert Pollard

"Lost at Gonesville Station"

I'm not speaking for the entire band because I wouldn't say it was a great show. I was far too nervous for it to be one of my better performances. I think it was part of the CMJ new music seminar in maybe 1994, and it was at the behest of Scat Records owner Robert Griffin who signed us in '93. We hadn't performed on stage in six years, and Robert told me that this particular showcase in New York City could do a great deal to enhance our profile as an "up-and-coming" band—the "real" band that we had now become, having signed to a "real" indie rock label. Also "up-and-coming" even though we were all around thirty-five years old at the time and had been playing in bands for close to twenty years. Before Scat, it was all make believe with six vanity-pressed LPs on make-believe labels.

Since I had agreed to play our first show in six years, I was all set to the task of assembling an official lineup for the gig, as Guided By Voices had just been a loose conglomeration of whoever decided to pop in during a recording session to that point. The lineup ended up being Tobin Sprout, Mitch Mitchell, Kevin Fennel, and Dan Toohey. We had the look, at the time, of a fairly typical, generic Ohio garage/punk band. We had started to garner some acclaim from the indie rock press and obscure cognoscente as these mysterious, lo-fi weirdos with an affectation for the Who/Beatles/British Invasion/Flying Nun Records. Our look was not only incongruous within the infrastructure of the band but also with most anything going on in the indie rock scene at the time. Some of us had long hair, some of us had short hair, one or two wore baseball hats. There may have even been dreadlocks or a mullet.

The show was at CBGB, and we were third of a five-band Scat/Thrill Jockey Records showcase. As I mentioned before, I was horrified almost to the point of physical sickness. It was a total schmooze fest in front of the club with indie rock luminaries, label people, and press co-mingling. Sonic Youth and Pavement were there. I was greatly concerned that we were about to be revealed as the clueless, talentless Midwestern hicks that I thought we very much had the potential to be labeled, as there was a reason for not having played live in six years. At the merchandise table, we sold a pink tank top with a purple octopus on the front (which to my surprise, ended up selling very well). Indigenous New Yorkers showed up wearing checkered shirts and cuffed jeans, anticipating what they thought might be the current, in-style trend for Southern Ohio lo-fi weirdo recording artists.

Before the show, during the aforementioned jerk fest, our drummer, Kevin, told me that he had approached Henry Rollins and said, "Hey, Henry—" to which Henry interrupted with a very angry and forceful *"What!"* Nothing against Henry, but I was like, "Why the fuck would you want to talk to Henry Rollins?" It just made me even more nauseous.

So we come on at around 10:00 p.m. with our baseball hats, Les Pauls, and white corduroys and gave it a go. I knew of only one confidence builder other than the alcohol I had been drinking all day and that was the fact that a few of us—at least Mitch Mitchell and I—were pretty decent athletes. We could move, jump, kick... drink. We both had a heavy-metal background, having been in a band in high school called Anacrusis.

So that's what we decided to do. Drink more. Move a lot. Kick out the set at a very brisk pace (I think it was a forty-five minute set) without much time between songs. Only the count—very Ramones style. I wasn't focusing on the crowd, just sort of gazing over the top of their heads at the exit sign in the back of the room because that's where I initially wanted to go. They seemed to be getting into it. What weirded me out and caused a huge surge of insecurity and paranoia was, about two-thirds of the way through the set, a pretty large portion of the crowd, maybe forty or fifty of them, began raising their cigarette lighters and yelling. I mistook it as a possible form of mockery or big city snobbery. A sarcastic protest of our arena rock posturing perhaps. We had been jumping and kicking, and it was a pretty energetic performance throughout the entire set, mainly out of sheer nervous energy from stage fright. I was informed by a group of people that came backstage afterwards that the reaction with the lighters was a show of genuine appreciation for the songs and for the fact that we "rocked" instead of "shoe-gazed," which was quotidian in indie or alternative rock.

The next morning, we met British rock press legend Everett True, who greeted us in our hotel lobby in a bathrobe and house slippers for our very first interview. In the piece that he wrote for *Melody Maker* (or maybe *NME*) he called us "The last great American underground rock band."

That CBGB show started it all for us. We stayed in Manhattan for the next four days and got tangled up in the scene. I didn't call anyone, including my friends and family, the entire time we were there. I was lost at Gonesville Station, and life would never be the same after that. We never became KISS or the next Nirvana, but we're still kicking it out some twenty years later.

51

MOBY

Born Richard Melville Hall (his stage name based on the eponymous whale from his distant uncle Herman Melville's Moby Dick*), MOBY was instrumental in the early incarnations of house and dance music. In 1999, MOBY released his fifth album,* Play, *which went on to sell over ten million records. "Porcelain" ended up selling millions more—the opener on that mix CD you regret making in college.*

My most embarrassing gig is not terribly dramatic, but it still pains me to think about it. I dropped out of college in 1984 and started a band with some friends. We were called AWOL, which was an acronym for Angels Without Light, because we were Joy Division-obsessed, gothic, overly dramatic suburban kids. We borrowed money from our parents and released this five-song EP, with the release party at a Chinese restaurant in Norwalk, Connecticut, called the D.C. Cafe. I have no idea why it was called that, but they were the only place that would allow us to set up equipment and play a show. I had a huge crush on a girl named Margaret Fiedler, who, oddly enough, has gone on to have a very interesting career in music. She was PJ Harvey's guitar player, and now she plays guitar in Wire.

I really wanted to impress her, so I invited her to our album release show at the D.C. Cafe, which was in a strip mall. It was the lowest of the lowest rung of Chinese restaurants. We set up, with our little borrowed PA, in the far corner next to some vegetable crates. We had made hundreds of flyers to promote the show and put them up in every record store and venue in the area. I had visions in my head of hundreds of people filling the restaurant. Margaret arrived shortly after by herself. The owner demanded that, in order for her to sit and watch the show, she had to order food. My friend Paul arrived with his cousin, and they were told the same thing. And, that was it. Literally no one else came to our show. This was our big, triumphant, record-release show, and the setting was so sad. There I was, trying to impress the girl that I had this huge crush on, playing sad songs in an empty Chinese restaurant, while she ate food that she'd been forced to order. Thankfully, Margaret and I still keep in touch to this day.

The craziest gig is going to sound like I'm overdramatizing this, or indulging in hyperbole, but I promise I'm not. With most shows, there's a little bit of chaos. But for this one, it was so insane that it was almost like scripted chaos. This was in 1997, and I was playing a festival at Leeds in the north of England. This was at a very low point for me professionally. I had just released an album called *Animal Rights* that no one liked. I was still playing the occasional festival, and I would try and play some of my new punk rock songs from *Animal Rights*, but in order to get paid, I had to play dance music, because that's what I was hired to do.

We started playing, and the audience was weirdly chaotic. It seemed like they had been drinking and taking drugs for a few days, which was probably the case. I played Woodstock '99, and this had a similar vibe of things just being wrong. Early into our set, I jumped into the audience. One of the security guards, who was either mentally ill or simply didn't realize that I was an artist, just started punching me. He was huge, and the audience was trying to pull me into the crowd while security was trying to pull me towards the stage. It didn't make any sense, because even if I was some kid who'd stage-dived, the security guard had no reason to start punching.

My arms were immobilized by the audience, and the security guards had my legs, while this guy was punching my head and back. Finally, I was somehow released, and I screamed in the guy's face. He hauled back to punch me again, and I ran back on stage. This has never happened before or since, but at that moment, I swear to you...my amplifier caught on fire and exploded. I'm not sure if it was a *Firestarter* moment, where my chaos and rage caused the amp to blow up, but there was fire belching out of the amp. I was muddy, bruised and bloody, and I started berating the violent security guard from the stage. He tried to get on stage, and my tour manager and the other guards literally had to wrestle him to the ground. Immediately after the last note of our set—and I swear I'm not kidding—the heavens opened up, and it was the biggest thunderstorm I've ever seen. It was biblical, and it felt...perfect.

52

WYCLEF JEAN

Did you know Wyclef is an accomplished mixed martial artist? Or that he performed with a lion on stage? Well, read all about it! One time, or two times.

One of the most embarrassing was with the Fugees. It was our first time playing Japan, and we were playing this huge stadium. We were introduced to sake. I didn't know what it was, and to me and Pras, the shit looked just like water. We drank sake until we couldn't drink sake no more and totally underestimated its power. The stage for our show was elevated about ten feet off the floor, so the crowd was below us. We opened with "Ready or Not," and I was looking for Pras, who was nowhere to be found. He was so drunk that he had fallen off the stage. I was dizzy, wobbly, and felt like hurling. Lauryn didn't drink. She was the smart one. There was no worse feeling, but I couldn't escape. I had to keep it going with the crowd, who were going crazy because they thought Pras tumbling off stage was part of the show. I was about to throw the fuck up all over that stage the entire set. It was the worst, but also kinda cool.

There's been violence at our shows. We got into a scuffle in Germany, and I had to fight. I'm a really nice guy, which makes me a great fighter, because I fight calm. This was sometime in the early '90s when promoters would pack shows with 6,000 kids. Hip-hop had just started coming, and we were having problems with some skinheads that night. After the show, they came at us with a vibe on the street, and we got into it. I had to whoop some ass. I grew up watching Royce Gracie, and I fell in love with the UFC when I was nineteen, before it was even the UFC. I love the art of fighting and mixed martial arts. I will never instigate violence unless it's in the act of self-defense. That night in Germany, I felt that we were being threatened. If you watch my video "The Ring," you'll see how I fight. They hit the fucking ground.

I'm a showman. I play with a sixty-four-piece orchestra. People don't know that I performed off-Broadway when I was younger. I love theatrics and putting shows together. One of my craziest shows as a soloist was when I was working with the artist Canibus, who was a battle rapper. He said to me, "I wanna be the hardest rapper. I want people to fear me." I said, "That's cool. In order for them to fear you, we gotta show up on stage with an uncaged lion. If you're rapping fearlessly with a lion, it doesn't get more hardcore than that."

I got introduced to big cats by Mike Tyson, who was moving with three cats at the time. They were in his house. When I was younger, I was obsessed with the circus. I was flipping off trampolines, doing gymnastics, and breakdancing. That was my culture. I was also obsessed with animals and had a sensitivity towards them. I felt like the fucking *Jungle Book* with them. For the song,

"2nd Round Knockout," we brought the lion out on stage with no cage. We didn't sedate the lion or anything because I love animals. When I say cat, I'm not talking about a baby Siamese. This was a full-blown, massive lion.

This was on the Smokin' Grooves Tour in 1998, and I always believe in bringing the arena the show. Even during the Fugees, I was always the one who would coordinate the show because I have big vision and imagination as a showman. That was one of the most memorable on-stage memories. If you talk to Busta Rhymes or Q-Tip for this book, they'll be like, "Yo, Wyclef came out with a fucking lion. Ain't no topping that." We had two trainers on stage for the lion. One night, the lion got loose, but my bodyguard Beast was able to control it. The lion was a little frustrated, but we were able to contain it. The lion was totally cool most of the time.

This was a professional show lion, so it wasn't like I went to the jungle and snatched him up. I don't know if PETA is against brothers, because it was just like watching the circus or going to the zoo. Every level of proper code was followed. You don't just bring a wild lion to a venue, so we respected and followed every protocol. No one was offended because the lion was not used in any way that was cruel or dealt with in any way that could be considered animal cruelty. It was the circus on stage. It was dope.

53

BRANDON BOYD

(Incubus)

Apart from my lack of talent, I could never be in a touring band. I have enough trouble falling asleep in my own bed, let alone tour buses and motels. I also curl up in a fetal position when sick and avoid the world. Brandon Boyd has one solution to fighting illness: alcohol.

Thankfully, for the purposes of this book, I have a lot of horror stories. One of the worst for me was when we did the Outside Lands Festival in San Francisco in 2009, a huge event in Golden Gate Park, with about 50,000 people. It was our first time playing the festival. We were so excited to do it, and we had just come off a super duper, and very well-attended, US tour. One of the worst things that can happen to a singer is to get sick, and there's a long history of hypochondriac lead singers as a result of the paranoia of getting a common cold. The day before the fest, I came down with a really nasty cold. I sort of felt OK, but my voice was completely trashed. I did everything in my power the day of the show to not freak out, but when I went to warm up my voice, there was just nothing there. I could barely talk. It was one of those situations where I wanted to just run away. I was praying for a UFO to abduct me or just something to get me as far away from that festival stage as possible.

I started to feel a panic attack coming on, thinking that I had less than an hour before I had to go out in front of all these people. Our bass player saw me pacing in the dressing room and asked if I was all right. I pointed to my throat and croaked, "I got no voice." Just before we went on stage, he grabbed a fresh bottle of wine, handed it to me, and said, "All right man, it's time to get drunk." For a lightweight like me, I downed a bottle and was properly drunk halfway through the set. I still couldn't sing a note, but I just didn't really care. I think at some point I announced to the crowd, in a drunken stupor, "Sorry Outside Lands, I'm fucking sick." I knew in my heart that it was one of the worst concerts I'd ever performed, and I could see by the tens of thousands of faces that they knew it too. They picked up on my I-don't-care-let's-get-drunk vibe, so people weren't booing. I don't remember much, but I do remember having fun, which was amazing considering how completely panicked I had been.

The catch is that we travel all over the world and make our living by touring. Out of all the shows we've done, the one I get the most feedback about is that goddamn Outside Lands show. I'll meet someone and after explaining that I'm the singer in Incubus, they'll say, "Oh, I saw you one time in San Francisco." I'll ask, "Oh cool, at the Warfield?" They say, "No, it was at Outside Lands."

That happens everywhere we go. I've met people in Abu Dhabi who saw the show. For the rest of my life, I'll have people coming up to me, saying they saw the worst show of my life.

In 2001, we put out an album called *Morning View,* and we had two sold-out dates set up at Hammerstein Ballroom in New York City to start the tour. It was a really exciting time for us, and there was all this lovely momentum coming off our last record *Make Yourself.* I woke up in my SoHo hotel room on September 11, which was just a few blocks away from the Twin Towers. We were close enough that when the planes hit the building, all the car alarms were going off below us, and my hotel window was rattling. It was viscerally shocking before I even had any idea what was going on. It was the most frightening experience I can remember having in my life. We played a show in New Hampshire on the thirteenth, and there was a strange, solemn mood the entire show. The next two shows were scheduled at Hammerstein on the fourteenth and fifteenth.

We were really uncertain about what was the right thing to do. We wanted to be there and play but also to be as respectful as possible. We considered canceling, and we asked the promoter what was going on. He said, "Everyone's canceling, but we're not telling any of the bands to cancel. We think some people may want to take their minds off things right now and come together." They ended up being two of the most memorable concerts in my professional life. There were moments where it was solemn and moments when it was extremely sad, but for the most part, there was a feeling of incredible unity and solidarity. I'm still really grateful that people came out, and a lot of people didn't show up. Both nights, the room was about three-quarters full, which was surprising, given the circumstances.

I've never heard an American audience sing as loud, or emote as freely, as on those two nights. It still sticks with me. It felt like the first step in a massive healing. Now, it seems like every couple of months, some nightmarish tragedy occurs at concerts, like the Vegas shooting. We had a residency lined up in Vegas at that time, and we did end up canceling that. It's such a strange feeling now to be a traveling entertainer in a world where weird, fucked-up stuff happens all the time, and I have to make that a part of my reality. I have this kind of hyper-vigilance now, and the shock and reality of these mass shootings doesn't wear off, nor should it. I don't want it to, and I don't want to normalize this reality. I don't want to resign myself to thinking, "Oh, well, people die at concerts now." I can't do that.

54

MERLE ALLIN

(GG Allin and the Murder Junkies)

So, it's come to this: The GG Allin chapter. His brother and former band-mate, Merle, is a really nice guy because, going in, I didn't know what to expect. Hold your noses everyone, here's a look into the brutality, human feces, nudity, heroin, and death that was the GG Allin experience.

Let's go back to 1991 and the first tour we did with GG. Knowing what to expect, but to actually have it happen while you're playing and watching it all unfold in front of you, is a totally different fucking story. Today, you can watch all the video of those performances you want, and it's not even a tenth of what was actually happening if you were there. This story is legendary in San Diego. It was a place called the Spirit Club, and the floor was set up with tables and chairs in a kind of sit down and watch a show formation. Normally, what I would do with the club owners or the promoters in charge of the show, was go to them behind GG's back before the show. I said to the Spirit Club owners, "This is what could happen. You should really put away these tables and chairs. Also, you should really serve alcohol in plastic cups tonight."

The owner just looked at me and laughed. He said, "No, no, it's fine. I've had Black Flag and such-and-such here before." He kept naming bands while shrugging off my warning. I said, "Well, that's your decision. But you'd be wise to move all your tables and chairs." He didn't heed my warning. A couple hours later we got on stage, start to play, and before long, the entire place looked like the fight scene of some old Western movie. Tables and chairs were flying all over the place. I think this show is the most scared I've ever been on stage. Bottles and chairs were flying at the stage, breaking all around my head. If someone on that stage said, "I wasn't scared!" man, you weren't fucking alive and breathing.

It was a goddamn war zone. GG was hanging off one of the water pipes, and he ended up breaking it. There was water, beer, shit, and blood all over the place. We actually ended up getting through most of the set. It was the craziest show I was ever a part of. If you talk about GG and San Diego, someone will say, "You remember the Spirit Club from '91?" We would always go to the shows early, and people loved hanging out with us until GG got drunk. Once GG got on stage, it went from a love to hate relationship real fast. People that were loving us and buying us drinks before the show, were the people throwing shit at our vans, breaking windows, and slashing our tires.

GG's protection from the crowd was covering himself with his own feces. He figured that nobody would touch him when he was covered in shit, and he was right. When he was covered in shit and throwing it into the crowd, it was kind of like his armor. GG's pre-game ritual was just getting as drunk as possible. His attitude and craziness depended on how long we had to wait before a show and how much he was able to drink during that time. We had a show in Joplin, Missouri, in 1993, which was our last tour with GG. It was in the middle of nowhere. We got to the show really early, probably earlier than we should have. There were too many bands on the bill and, back then, we never traveled with any equipment. We realized after the first tour that traveling with equipment was the worst thing we could do because we'd always have to flee the club with amps, drums, and guitars on our backs. People would already have smashed our shit anyway during the show.

After that first tour, it was always prearranged that one band on the bill would have to supply us with equipment, and we still do that to this day. So, we're backstage in Joplin, and GG was getting really antsy. When GG wanted to do something, you had better be ready to go, or he was going to leave you behind. Or he might do something far worse. The band whose equipment we were set to use was onstage playing. We had already been paid, as I made it a point to always try and get paid before we played. All the shit that GG would break during the show would otherwise be deducted from our pay.

As we were waiting forever backstage, GG was pacing while getting more anxious and pissed off. He was like a caged animal that was drinking and getting fucked up. I could see that he was ready to explode. Suddenly, GG runs out of the dressing room, jumps on stage, and tackles the lead singer. He threw the guy to the ground, knocked over all the equipment, and barked, "You guys are fucking done!" Yep, they were done. The whole fucking show was done, and we didn't even get to play. At this point, it started to become a mob scene. We had already gotten paid, and we weren't giving our fucking money back. We told our driver to get the van, and we planned to get out as discretely as possible, as the band GG attacked obviously wasn't going to let us use their equipment anymore.

We all piled into the van, and the next thing we know, there were four or five vehicles following us down the highway. We were driving and saying, "Fuck man, there's a goddamn mob after us." Finally, after miles of being tailed, we said, "Fuck these assholes! Let's pull over and see what they fucking do." We pulled over, they slowed down, and after getting one look at us, they peeled off in the opposite direction. They did not want to fuck with us.

Another really bad one was from 1991 in New York City. Todd Phillips was filming for the documentary *Hated*. We knew the show was going to be on film, so GG was primed to go. A week before the show, I had to meet with the owner and booking agent to sign a bunch of papers. I was signing off on all this shit, basically promising in writing that GG wouldn't do this or that. The whole time I was signing and making these promises, I was thinking, "This is insane. This is never gonna happen." I always played along, saying that GG would behave and everything would be fine. The club we were slated to play was really small. The room with the stage was decent size, but there was a bottleneck to get out. It was only about two or three people wide, and that spelled trouble.

Night of the show, Todd had the cameras set up, and GG was getting really fired up. Everyone was excited to play, and the place was fucking packed. Because of the cameras, I knew it was going to be an all-out GG attack. Sure as shit, after the first line of the first song "Bite It You Scum," GG busted this poor kid in the face. As soon as GG cracked that kid in the face and broke his nose, blood sprayed everywhere. People freaked out and ran for the exit. It was mayhem, and people were stomping all over each other. GG ended up breaking two kids' noses that night. The show lasted about two and a half songs, and the cops barged in as we were singing "Kill the Police." GG made his escape that night, but the club Space and Chase closed down shortly after.

Because GG died of a heroin overdose, the biggest misconception is that he was a junkie. The fact is he rarely ever did heroin. It was just something he did when it was available to him or when he was around someone who did it. Sure, GG would do any drug, but he was mostly just a heavy drinker. I think the fact that he rarely did heroin was one of the contributing factors to his death.

If GG was hanging out, chilling with my wife and I in my house, he was as normal as you and I doing this interview. He was a really smart guy and a fucking genius at writing songs. I couldn't have asked for a greater brother, and that's the truth. We grew up together knowing we wanted to play music. We were best friends. He was great in an atmosphere with just his close friends and not out in public being GG. As soon as he got out with people and fans he didn't personally know, he had to outdo everyone. The people that tried to outdo him, he would totally explode on. The people that actually approached and talked to him after a show who weren't total assholes, he was totally cool with them. But because of the stage show and the violence, everyone assumed that he would have been a dick or smacked them in the head if they tried to talk to him. Eventually, I'm going to write a book about my whole fucking experience with GG.

55

JON WURSTER

(Superchunk/Bob Mould Band)

I have a man-crush confession: Jon Wurster is my favorite drummer. He also has great hair. Wurster submitted this chapter to me about the very surreal night that he backed Katy Perry at the 2009 MTV Video Music Awards.

Written by Jon Wurster

I was walking my dog in Brooklyn one rainy Thursday morning when I received a phone call from a fellow musician. He asked if I'd be interested in joining a small cadre of drummers he was putting together to back Katy Perry at that Sunday's MTV Video Music Awards at Radio City Music Hall. Though I was fully embedded in the indie rock world and had not watched MTV for at least a decade, I agreed immediately because this was just too bizarre an opportunity to pass up. Also, the only thing I had on tap for that weekend was a solo excursion to a matinee screening of Matt Damon's new film *The Informant!*

The next day I reported to a rehearsal studio on Manhattan's West Side. On hand were three other drummers, our Musical Director (who would be playing a full drum kit), and a young Izzy Stradlin-looking guitarist. The MD informed us that we'd be adding percussive support for Katy as she opened the VMA's with Queen's classic 1976 hit "We Will Rock You." If you know the song, you know that any Neanderthal with a club can pound out its *Boom-Boom-Thwack* cadence, but apparently they needed professional Neanderthals to do it right, so there we were.

Two timpani and two large bass drums were positioned in front of a little stage in the rehearsal room. I was hoping to play timpani, but the MD put me on bass drum duty. Anyone who's played percussion in their school band knows the bass drum is the instrument of shame—the equivalent of your Little League coach stationing you in left field. I wasn't going to let it get me down though. This was going to be a memorable experience, and I was going to whack that bass drum like it owed me at least forty dollars.

As it turned out, Queen was allowing MTV use of the original stomps, claps, and backing vocals straight from their *News of the World* album master tapes. This made the experience extra special because my brother Lane and I used to scare ourselves silly listening to "We Will Rock You" as we stared at the murderous giant robot that graced *News of the World*'s cover. Also, Queen's 1980 concert at the Philadelphia Spectrum was the first big arena show I ever attended. Every time I smell marijuana, I still think of the two shirtless dirtbags who marched around the upper-tier cheap seats yelling "Who wants to fuckin' get high?"

Katy soon breezed in with a small retinue of assistants and managers. She introduced herself to everybody and then turned to me and said, "You look familiar." "Oh, I've been around," I replied. It was a weird thing to say, and I don't blame her for not really speaking to me again. We got down to business and ran through the song a handful of times, the five drummers pounding out rhythm while Katy found her way with the vocal. Young Izzy nailed Brian May's iconic solo note-for-note and everything felt pretty good by the final run-through.

The next day we assembled at Radio City Music Hall for an onstage rehearsal. I'd played Radio City eleven years earlier, opening for John Fogerty as a member of Ryan Adams's band Whiskeytown, but this was a whole different animal. This was live, star-studded national television. Rehearsal was running a little late, so I explored the theater, wandering amongst empty seats reserved for the likes of Beyoncé, Pink, and Taylor Swift. I took a selfie in front of a chair set aside for astronaut Buzz Aldrin because that was the weirdest one I could find.

We settled into place behind our drums on the big stage and banged through "We Will Rock You." It was pretty thrilling to be up there, and the drums, Katy, and Izzy's guitar solo sounded great. But there was one hitch: MTV wanted a "name" guitarist to play the solo. I really felt for our young gunslinger. He learned the solo perfectly and sounded wonderful playing it. But he was guilty of an unforgivable crime: He wasn't famous.

The usual suspects were tossed around: Slash, Dave Navarro, etc., but MTV was having difficulty nailing down a star guitarist. It was a lot to ask a well-known, already established guitar hero to come in on almost no notice and risk crashing and burning in front of millions of people on live TV. At some point that Saturday, news came that Aerosmith guitarist Joe Perry had accepted the challenge and would fly to New York City the next morning and play the VMAs that night.

So there we were Sunday morning, back at the west side rehearsal studio at the very un-rock 'n' roll hour of 10:00 a.m. The door to the rehearsal room was closed, and we were told we could not yet enter. Ten or so minutes later, we were given the OK to come in and there he was: Joe Perry, looking as much like Joe Perry as anyone has ever looked like Joe Perry. The first four Aerosmith albums were the soundtrack to my junior high years, so playing with Joe Perry, even if I was just banging on a bass drum, was a very big deal for me.

One of my favorite family trips occurred in the fall of 1978 when my dad booked a room at the south Philadelphia Hilton for us to hang out and spend the night in while Lane saw Aerosmith at the aforementioned Spectrum. Lane returned much earlier than expected due to Aerosmith singer Steven Tyler being hit in the face with shards of a glass bottle someone threw onstage. A similar incident involving a firecracker to the face forced the band to abandon their Spectrum show a year earlier. When my brother came back to our hotel room he excitedly told us that Aerosmith drummer Joey Kramer stormed up to Tyler's mic and bellowed, "You got a real problem, Philadelphia!" Now there's something I think we can all agree on.

The sound Joe and his tech were getting in the rehearsal room was the polar opposite of the classic, raunchy Joe Perry guitar crunch the world knows and loves. The clean, distortion-less tone coming out of the amp would not have been out of place on a Dead Milkmen album (hey, I'm from Philly, so my references are regional). Joe was working with an unfamiliar amp, and it was ten in the morning, so this was understandable.

Halfway into our first pass at the song it became apparent Joe had never actually played the solo in his life. And why would he have? He's Joe fucking Perry, author of many of rock 'n' roll's greatest riffs and solos. He's a creator, not a tribute artist. But it threw a little monkey wrench into the proceedings. Joe's solo was inspired and original, but it wasn't the "We Will Rock You" solo. Also, it was way too long. This would be a major issue, as we would soon find out.

When the song was over we all shot each other confused glances. At one point a member of Katy's management team turned to me and nervously asked, "This will be OK, won't it?" The turn of events was most unexpected, so I couldn't give him a definitive answer. Unfortunately, there was no time to go over the song again because we were due over at Radio City for a full-production rehearsal. At RCMH we were told we'd be carried up from below the stage on one of the theater's hydraulic lifts. This was very cool because it would allow me to live out a long-dormant childhood fantasy of taking the stage as KISS did on their 1979 Dynasty tour. I would not be allowed to spit blood at any point, but that was OK.

"We Will Rock You" was the first musical performance of the night and would also serve as the entrance for VMA host Russel Brand. Russell would descend a flight of stairs, make his way out onto the runway, and bask in applause while Joe played his guitar solo. Joe's solo needed to be over at a specific time in order for the show to remain on schedule. This was crucial.

We ran through the song and everything was on track until the guitar showcase. Joe soloed out onto the runway where he wailed away among a sea of seats that would soon be filled by celebrities and beautiful people. The song ended with Joe still soloing on the runway and Russell looking perplexed about what should happen next. This was not good.

Make no mistake, nobody has ever looked cooler playing a guitar than Joe Perry, and his performance at soundcheck was no exception. But the length of the solo was causing heart attacks among the people running the show. The MD was taken aside by panicked network representatives and told there were hundreds of thousands of dollars of at stake if the song ran long and cut into a commercial. Exhausted and in need of sleep, Joe headed back to his nearby hotel room.

While I explored Radio City Music Hall (at one point sharing an elevator with a masked, stage-blood-spattered Lady Gaga) the MD tried in vain to reach Joe by phone to get with him about the length of the solo. Hours later he eventually connected with Joe and impressed upon him the importance of keeping it to a specific number of bars. The new plan was for the MD to play an elongated drum roll to signal the end of the song. There would now be no mistaking when we all should stop playing.

Few of the VMA's big stars were on hand for that afternoon's run-through, so I was absolutely shocked when a familiar face came into my field of vision just as the lights went down at show time. "Holy fuck, that's Madonna," I said to myself as she glided by me. The Material Woman gracefully ascended a flight of stairs and took her place at the landing just above me where she waited in the dark for her introduction. It still stands as one of the most surreal moments of my life—hocking spit into my hands to ensure a secure bass drum mallet grip while watching Madonna silently prepare to walk into a spotlight and deliver a tribute to the recently deceased Michael Jackson.

I find that when you play on live TV, you go into a weird kind of shock. My friend and bandmate Bob Mould likens it to running out onstage and boxing somebody for three minutes while holding a guitar. This experience was no different. We rode the hydraulic lift to stage level, the MD counted off the song, and that's the last thing I remember.

Today, thanks to the Space Age miracle of the internet, I watched our performance for the first time in nine years. I was honestly surprised how good it is. Katy struts the stage confidently, Joe reels off a barrage of cool guitar fills, and we drummers hammer away (without dropping our sticks) as an arena-rock light show swirls around us. There's no evidence of the uncertainty we were all experiencing regarding the song's ending—the kind of uncertainty you feel watching a scene in a thriller where someone is tasked with defusing a bomb by cutting one of two wires.

The video, however, reveals a somewhat less dramatic conclusion. Joe sticks close to center stage as he plays a blistering solo. Russell stalks the runway, looking back a couple times to see if Joe is wrapping up his solo. He isn't, he's still blazing. But then Joe goes into the main finale riff, and we're back on track. The big drum roll happens and, somehow, none of us stop at the same time!

The song skids and tumbles to a halt that sounds like the ending of every live Rolling Stones song before they got pro on 1989's Steel Wheels tour.

The drummers immediately returned to our dressing room to recover from those two minutes of glory. Questions abounded: "Did we end it right?" "Could you hear the drum roll?" "Was that Vin Diesel in the second row?" Sadly, while we compared notes, we missed the most infamous event to ever occur at the VMAs: Kanye West's hijacking of Taylor Swift's Moonman. It would have been nice to one day tell my grandchildren I witnessed it in person.

We never saw Joe Perry, Katy Perry, or Russell Brand again that night. Russell saw a lot of Katy in the ensuing days, tying the knot with her months later for what would be a tumultuous two-year marriage. Joe Perry continues to be the greatest Joe Perry anybody could possibly be. Our musical director, relieved to have the preceding three days in his rear-view mirror, kindly invited his rhythm partners to the RCMH bar for a post-performance drink. Unfortunately for me, I stopped drinking just a month before. I really could have used it. FYI: I went to see *The Informant!* on Monday. I liked it.

56

NICK HEXUM

(311)

They were several years older, but I grew up with 311 in Omaha. Conor Oberst also lived down the street, and I remember playing soccer in his backyard a few times. Anyway, here's front man Nick Hexum on marijuana and getting a boot in the face.

I call this my "Welcome to New Jersey" story. We were playing at this place called Convention Hall on the Asbury Park boardwalk. They've cleaned it up a lot over the years, but when we were playing it in the '90s, it was a ghost town. It's featured in The Sopranos, and I think it's where Big Pussy got killed. It's a beautiful, old, haunted stone building, and we would have the wildest shows there. The first time we played there, after the first note, the place erupted, and I got hit right in the face with a boot. Clocked me right in the nose. It came flying out of the mosh pit. It was one of those heavy, big-soled, '90s boots, and it was heavier than a Doc Marten.

I kept going, but I immediately thought, "This is gonna be a long fuckin' night. Welcome to New Jersey." I think they just call the boot-in-the-face a Jersey Hi-Five. It did take me a minute to recompose myself, and I had to also remember that I've thrown shit out of the mosh pit before. It's not necessarily that someone is mad or hates your band. It's not like a rotten tomato. It's just a kid who wants to get your attention and is having so much fun that they don't know how to contain themselves. Those Convention shows were always the craziest.

Our crowd has always been hard to peg. It's a blend of skaters, punks, and kids who liked weed, NOFX, Nirvana, Rage Against the Machine, Cypress Hill, and reggae. I've always thought of myself as more of a punk than a metalhead. The hardcore punks might listen to us and dismiss it as non-punk. To me, it's always been more about a punk attitude than sound. I don't have any tattoos, so I don't fit into the punk mold. It's an attitude that I learned from Joe Strummer, which is to do whatever the hell you want and not worry about categories. I think that people who sound like punk from twenty years ago are the real poseurs. When the Clash and Sex Pistols started, they sounded like something no one had ever heard before.

Here's a good embarrassing story. 311's marijuana anthem is a cover of a solo by H.R. from Bad Brains' song, "Who's Got the Herb?" We've never put it out on an album, but it did come out on a box set. When we play it live, that's when everyone pulls out the weed and lights up. There's a part in the breakdown late in the song where I try and act all cool, dancing around the stage and pointing to people in the audience, "Who's got it? Who's got it?" I'll usually include the name of the town, like, "Who's got it...here in Columbus!"

Normally when I yell the city, the crowd erupts. This time there was no reaction whatsoever. There was just a bunch of smoke clouds and people staring at me. I yelled Columbus, but we were actually in Cincinnati. It took me about ten seconds to realize I had fucked up. I was completely mortified, and talk about killing the vibe of the place during a pot anthem. I wasn't stoned, but considering we've done over 2,000 shows, you're gonna botch a city here and there. Bruce Springsteen has done it too...c'mon!

Weed has always been a part of our creativity. Being rebellious kids, it was something we fell into during our Omaha days. You can imagine how hard it was for us to score and find halfway decent stuff back then. It was mostly ditch weed that would give us headaches. Cannabis has come so far in my lifetime. Now, I have more than I could ever deal with. I'm in the industry—I grow it, and I also make vapes. From the beginning, that was our process. We'd smoke and put a song together, and that hasn't changed. I don't like to be really stoned on stage because I've gotta be really extroverted. In the studio or hanging out with the guys and practicing—that's the best cannabis time for me.

I'll always remember this one too. It was back on the first tour we ever did, and it was a straight-up mess. First, we had an RV fire. Everything burned up, and we lost all our equipment. We borrowed some money to buy a new RV and drove up to Vancouver for a show. We were so excited about going international, and as soon as we crossed the border, an axle on our new RV broke. We probably had about 150 bucks between us to make it to the show, and a new axle, with labor, cost about 3,000 bucks. The part wasn't available in Canada, so we had to wait a week to have it shipped to us.

It was a total nightmare, but we found a really nice Canadian family who let us stay with them. We only had that one show in Vancouver, and when we finally got there, we were so stressed out that we collectively decided to go berserk. We were drinking so hard before the show, and kept right on into the show. We gave this insane performance where we were rolling around on the stage, and we whipped the place into a fury. It's one of the wildest shows I can remember, just jumping off shit and drinking into oblivion. 1994 at the Town Pump. If video exists, it's probably nowhere near as good as I remember it.

57

LOUIS PÉREZ

(Los Lobos)

True lifers, Los Lobos is close to entering their fiftieth year as a band. If you've never heard the album Kiko, *I implore you to check it out while reading this chapter. Here, drummer/multi-instrumentalist Pérez talks navigating the East LA punk scene and a very uncomfortable David Letterman appearance.*

As musicians, we all go through the wringer. The good gigs aren't necessarily memorable, but musicians can always remember the most embarrassing or completely disastrous gigs. Los Lobos has been a band for over forty-four years, so we've seen everything. 1980 was the year that we crossed the LA river to start playing clubs in the punk, New Wave scene that was happening in Hollywood. I had just made friends with Tito Larriva from the Latino punk band the Plugz, who went on to be the music guy in a bunch of Robert Rodriguez movies.

Before we crossed the river, we had basically been playing traditional Mexican music in East Los Angeles. Los Lobos were all rock 'n' roll kids growing up, and we became buddies in high school. We learned some traditional songs to play for our parents on one of our Mom's birthdays. That's where the seed was planted, and we were hooked on the greatness of traditional musicianship. We put away the Strats, amps, and Fenders to play traditional for the next ten years.

As my friendship with Tito grew, I became more interested in what was happening in the rock and punk scene on the other side of town. When we discovered the Blasters and what they were doing with rock, that was when we knew we had to change up the traditional thing. One day Tito called, saying that a band had dropped out from a gig he was doing. It was a slot opening for PIL, Johnny Rotten's band, at the Olympic Auditorium in downtown LA, which was an old wrestling arena.

We jumped at the chance, as we knew who the Sex Pistols were, but it was also just a great opportunity to get seen. This was like the second coming of the punk messiah Johnny Rotten, so it was a big deal in LA. We were so excited, and as I've thought about it over the years, I don't know if Tito set us up for failure. We were the first band playing, and the crowd was ready to sink their teeth into any band that wasn't PIL.

Right when we walked on stage, they threw every fucking thing imaginable at us. They didn't even give us a chance to plug in and see what we were about. They just wanted blood. I felt the rush of wind from all of the arms rising to give us middle fingers. It was a typical punk rock thing, but I was honestly surprised at some of the shit I saw fly on stage. They were spitting at us and throwing balled-up paper towels covered in God knows what.

We made it to the eight-minute mark, and that's when the really serious projectiles started flying. There was one guy on the side of the stage that was getting change from the bartender to throw nickels and quarters at us. He was aiming to sink one into the hole of our guitarrón, which is a big, six-string, Mexican bass. When it got to a point that wasn't exactly life-threatening, but close, we ran off the stage. We could have run back to East LA with our tail between our legs because we had invited all of our families to the show. They were hanging on the side of the stage, next to the spitters and the change-thrower.

When we ran off that stage, they were in tears. We all thought it was going to be our big break, so this was the worst thing that could have happened. But we just kept going. Instead of going back home and finding a day job, we had the resiliency of East LA chicanos that didn't let us quit. We were used to seeing gang fights and struggle back home, so this was just a minor speed bump. We stayed in touch and finally met the Blasters, who invited us to do a big show at the Whiskey a Go-Go. We were in, and the rest is history.

I don't think the response to us at the PIL show was racially-charged. That crowd was so amped because the Sex Pistols never made it to Los Angeles. They got as far as San Francisco and imploded. We went up there with acoustic instruments playing traditional Mexican music. We could have been a traditional Japanese Koto band, and it would have been just as strange to them. We never dwelt on how our race played into things. It turned out that one of the guys from the Blasters was at the show, and later he said that we were the bravest guys in the world to go up there in front of that crowd and play what we did.

That night is so important to me because it was our introduction to a new world. Circle Jerks and Black Flag was happening, and we all used to go to Madame Wong's after gigs to hang out. Darby Crash would walk in and literally have to duck down because his mohawk was too high to fit through the door. It was a magical time, and we made friends with all those people. If we would have run home that night, nothing would have happened.

There was a dark side to punk, with drugs and that shit. I don't think it was just endemic to punk though. It was rampant at that time in early '80s Los Angeles. We'd play weekend gigs and party afterwards. But once we started seriously touring, we all had to put the brakes on. We made the decision to become rock stars as adults, so we were older than most of the people on the scene. Darby Crash was just a kid, and I was twenty-nine when our first record came out. I would say that we had more sense than everybody else, but I don't think that's possible in rock 'n' roll.

One time we were performing on the David Letterman show, sometime in the mid-'90s. We did sound check, and David said hello before the show. We were in the green room, and the production assistant was explaining about our monitors and what was going to happen during the show. We were watching the show live, and Dave did his monologue and usual schtick. This was a "Stupid Human Tricks" night, where people would come out and show off some goofy, unusual trick.

One of the acts was this little kid, who was maybe eight years old. I can't remember exactly what his trick was, but he walked on stage, and Dave started interviewing him. "Hi, how old are you? Where are you from?" It was light pleasantries. The kid lived on a farm down South somewhere. Let's just call the kid Timmy for now. Dave said, "So Timmy, you live on a farm. What's a typical day on the farm?" Timmy said, in this cute Southern accent, "Well, I get up in the morning and have my breakfast. Sometimes I go in the field and help the Mexicans pick peppers."

There was an awkward silence, but Letterman was a pro and moved on. But it was very obvious to the audience and millions of viewers that it was a big, fucking oops. Dave was back at his desk after the bit, and before going to commercial, he said, "We'll be right back. Paul, can you check if Los Lobos are still here?" It became a running joke for the rest of the show until we went on. Before each commercial break, he'd turn to Paul and say, "Can you check on Los Lobos again?"

Right after it happened, the PA and a producer rushed back to see us. They were apologizing profusely, but we were never offended to begin with. It was just a kid from the South! He didn't mean it in some derogatory way. But man, Letterman's staff acted like that kid had cursed our mothers and spit in our faces. They were definitely squirming, and we felt bad for them. We're like, "Guys, we're cool. It's really no big deal."

Before we played, Letterman dedicated the song to the little kid. His people didn't stop apologizing to us until we left the building. It would have been funny if we had played it like we were extremely offended and locked the door to the green room.

58

DON BREWER

(Grand Funk Railroad)

Being a total Simpsons *nerd, I couldn't resist reaching out to a member of Homer Simpson's favorite band from the classic "Homerpalooza" episode. So, crank up the FM, turn on the blacklight, and spark up a doobie for Grand Funk!*

Let's go back to Honolulu, Hawaii, 1971. We were just a trio at the time, as we hadn't added a keyboardist yet. The big rage at the time was how good the pot was in Hawaii. Everyone wanted to get their hands on some Kona Gold. We arrived, but I wasn't a big pot smoker. I'd partake every now and then, but the other two guys in Grand Funk certainly were, and they got a bunch of it. They didn't try it out until before the show, which I knew was probably a mistake.

As we progressed through the show, I noticed that the music was getting worse and worse. By the time we got to our cover of the

Animals' "Inside Looking Out," which was our biggest song at the time, things went off the rails. There's a big, elongated guitar solo, with the bass and drums pumping, and you have to be pretty tight to pull it off. When we got to the big climax, my two bandmates got totally lost. We weren't used to that kind of pot back home, so it must have been like an acid trip for them.

Pretty soon, they started playing a completely different song, while I was still going on "Inside Looking Out." I had no idea what they were playing, as they were off on some other planet. You talk about Grand Funk Railroad having a train wreck, man...that was it. I just stopped playing, and they kept going. I just stood there, and eventually, they quit playing. Then, we just walked off the stage. It was not our finest moment, and it was my most embarrassing Grand Funk moment.

When I saw people going into bathrooms and using needles, I was smart enough to leave. I raised my daughter by saying, "I don't care if you go to a party. Just know when it's time to get the hell out." For us, it was the wild and crazy '70s, and groupies were the big thing. They were always trying to get backstage and hook up with the band. That was going on all the time. But I was the boring one. I was the one to always drive everyone home.

We didn't get sucked in by everything though. We stayed in Flint, Michigan, and didn't get caught up in everything by moving to New York or LA. There are so many ungodly stories about what happened to so many people and bands during that time. It's like being a football player and, eventually, it will end. There's not a ton of longevity, and there's a reason you don't see a bunch of guys like Elton John or Paul McCartney around. Very few people can be

Bruce Springsteen and make a lifelong career out of it. Most of the time, they're gonna come and go. When they go, it goes down hard. It goes down bad.

We avoided that, and I think we did a pretty good job. We were kind of outcasts. We were from Flint, and all of the "in" bands were from Ann Arbor or Detroit, like The Stooges and MC5. When Grand Funk finally got nationwide success, we were the last band to be accepted in our home state. They certainly didn't love us on the way up. So we just stayed to ourselves and did our own thing. We had a slow demise as disco came in. There was a lot of in-fighting about which direction we should go, and we were getting burned out on each other.

In 1976, we were working on an album with Frank Zappa, who was producing. We just couldn't get along, and we disbanded after. It really didn't come around until our music became classic rock in the '90s. All the labels started reissuing catalogs and classic rock stations were springing up everywhere. Classic rock became an institution, and we reunited in 1996. What's funny is that *The Simpsons* was instrumental in us reuniting because we are Homer Simpson's favorite band.

I co-wrote the song that *The Simpsons* wanted to use in the episode, which is "Shinin' On." They sent me the "Homerpalooza" script because they wanted to get our approval to use the song. In the episode, Homer is driving his kids to school and "Shinin' On" comes on the radio. Homer launches into this whole thing about how much he loves Grand Funk, and he's so shocked to learn that the kids don't know Grand Funk. He mentions each of us by name, and I thought it was a great use of the song and a really cool tribute to the band. We learned that one of the writers was a huge Grand Funk fan, and he's made Grand Funk references in numerous episodes.

We started having young kids and musicians referencing that episode after shows. After they are done asking about Homer, they'll say, "I didn't know you guys could rock like that!" Forty years on, and we're still doing great. We're not selling out arenas, but we're happy.

59

LITA FORD

Growing up in The Runaways, Lita Ford learned young and fast about rock 'n' roll excess, as the band used to party with Sid and Nancy on the group's French houseboat. She dishes on the '70s punk scene and about getting royally punked by Poison.

Because I'm a female, everything has been a goddamn fight. When The Runaways ended and I started my solo career, everything was crazy, and it was totally life-changing. I could have left music forever after The Runaways, but I chose to carry on. It's what I love to do and what I feel I was put on this earth to do. But from the start, it's always been crazy.

In The Runaways, there was always something really fucking dramatic going on, and it's why I hate drama so much today. One day, it would be Cherie Currie is sixteen and pregnant! Ah fuck, are you kidding me? What are we gonna do?

One time, we were in Japan, and Jackie desperately wanted to go home. She's a fucking hypochondriac and thought she was dying. We were like, "Dude, you are not dying! You can't go home because we still have to play Budokan!" So what did Jackie do? She slit her wrist with a broken plate from room service. She thought she was so sick that she attempted suicide to get a ticket home. That Budokan show was huge for us, and Joan Jett had to play bass. I covered on guitar, and it was fucking awesome. Nobody really missed Jackie that much, I'm sorry to say.

I remember the punk era as being really awesome, and it's probably my favorite era. If the fans loved you, they would spit on you. If you were in a club and the place was absolutely packed with a bunch of dudes in leather jackets, all you would see is spit flying through the air. It looked like it was raining sideways. When that big loogie would splash on my guitar neck, I just had to play through it. What are you gonna do, stop and get a fucking wet wipe? We all learned how to spit really well, and I loved it.

The very first tour The Runaways did was three months, across the US, with the Ramones. I had just come out of high school, and it was so badass. People would throw handfuls of change at us, and that shit hurt! The Ramones would put chicken wire in front of the stage to cut down on the spit and change. There was nothing fake about those guys. Joey looked fucked up, skinny, down-and-dirty nasty, and that's exactly who he was. He was truly one fucked-up individual but also a genius. They'd eat greasy fried chicken and then sing about wanting to get well. They should have eaten some vitamin C along with their heroin, Jack Daniels, and reds.

The Runaways had a ninety-foot house boat on the river Thames, next to the Battersea Bridge. Sid Vicious and Nancy would just walk right in. Sid would be drunk and fucking high as shit. He had just carved Nancy's name into his arm with razor blades, and his chest was bleeding with the word "Sid." He'd be dripping blood, his hair all matted from the night before. He was heavy duty, but I could have real conversations with him. But he was scary. When he'd start talking, I'd usually get up and walk away and go talk to Nancy. She was a doll. She was so gorgeous and a really sweet person. Then Sid would yell something, and it would snap me back to reality. I'd go in the other room and make peanut butter sandwiches for everyone. Everyone knew we had peanut butter sandwiches on the boat, so that's what brought everyone over. We didn't have paper plates, and nobody did dishes. Most of our plates got thrown out the window into the river.

That era was so raunchy, with people slicing themselves up with razor blades. The drugs were better back then, and I stayed together for a lot longer than people might realize. Blackberry brandy was my drug in The Runaways days. We'd be booked on these winter, outdoor festivals in Europe, and I was freezing. My fingers were so cold, and I had to go out and play guitar. My mother, being from Rome, and my father from Great Britain, said, "Lita! Have some blackberry brandy!" I used to carry a pint of it in the back pocket of my jeans. That was how the shit really started. From there, I went to Johnnie Walker Black Label. I loved alcohol and really had fun with it for a while. There was always so much different alcohol to try, and cocaine was always available. I didn't love coke at first, but I eventually got deeper into it. One day, I just said that I didn't want to do it anymore. I put all my drugs and alcohol into a box and put it out front for the trash man. That was in 1990 when my mother died. I had too much fun in the eighties.

One of the most embarrassing shows for me in the eighties was when I was on tour with Poison. I knew the guys in passing, but I didn't really hang out all night partying with them. At the end of the tour, I felt like I really hadn't gotten to know them, and I thought they went overboard with what they did to me on stage. It was the last night of the tour pranks, and I got really, really pissed. I don't know who exactly did it, but they duct-taped my guitar tech to a chair. While I was on stage, they lowered him from the rafters. He came down out of the sky, and I was pissed. I acted like I was laughing, but I wasn't happy. Then, during the show, they brought two male strippers onstage, who started flapping their penises on me. Whipped cream rained down, and I just lost it. I jumped off stage and into the orchestra pit to get away from these strippers.

Backstage, Poison were getting ready to go on. All of their keyboards were lined up, all nice and neat. All the programs, samples, and backing vocals were in the keyboards, and I kicked them over as hard as I could. I sent them flying and crashing to the ground. They had to go on in forty-five minutes, and I wiped out their samples. I looked over and saw C.C. DeVille's guitars lined up perfectly in a row. I figured that if I kicked one, it would have the domino effect, knocking the rest over. I lifted one foot and some-one grabbed me from behind. He wrapped his arms around mine and literally picked me up, moving me away from the guitars. It was Poison's tour manager. He was six foot four—a foot taller than me—so he picked me up like it was nothing. He's carrying me kicking and screaming through the backstage area, past Poison and all these crew people, trying to get me to my bus. My clothes and hair were totally covered in whipped cream, and I see Bret Michaels smiling and laughing. I just thought, "Fuck you," and I punched him as hard as I could in the mouth. Finally, the guy got me to my bus, and I had to think, *OK Lita, just get in and shut up.* We've actually become great friends over the years and still play together.

JOSH FREESE

Drummer Josh Freese has the coolest career, playing with everyone from DEVO to Nine Inch Nails. Perhaps closest to both our hearts are the decades he's spent with Paul Westerberg, solo, and in the brief reformation of The Replacements. In this love letter to our hero, Freese recounts an ill-fated MTV performance and the time he yelled "Burt Reynolds" on SNL.

There are artists that I grew up loving, like Paul Westerberg, that I would always daydream about meeting one day. Then I was suddenly in the studio working with him. In the early days, I really had to pretend like I wasn't starstruck by him, even though it was probably painfully obvious that I was freaking out.

In early summer 1993, Westerberg had just made his first solo record, *14 Songs*. We were in New York to play Irving Plaza, and we heard from the label that MTV wanted Paul to do a live performance with an interview for *120 Minutes*. He did the interview fine, but then it came to the performance, which was only going to be a couple songs. Paul said that he wanted the full band involved, as he didn't want to do it acoustic. Because our gear was across town being set up at Irving Plaza, MTV rented a really nice back-line for us, with a really nice drum set for me.

It turned into this really elaborate production. Since it was no longer just a guy on a stool with one mic and acoustic guitar, they had to set up a stage in the studio. They had to bring in monitors, extra camera guys, and all this shit that MTV hadn't anticipated, and had to assemble it in record time. It was a big, expensive deal. It was under the guise that Paul would perform, and they would take one or two of the songs to put into heavy rotation. The truth is, it was going to be a great thing for Paul, in terms of exposure.

We get to the studio, and there was all this buzz in the hall-ways. LA people from Warner Brothers had flown out. There were a ton of excited label people hanging out and people from MTV who had shown up to watch. We rehearsed and did a sound check, then had to do all the camera blocking shit. It was hectic—a lot of hurry up and wait. All of this, of course, is that absolute shit that Paul hates more than anything. Paul is the last guy to say, "Wow, look at all the label people. I can't wait to be on TV, isn't this great?"

Paul started grumbling, wondering what he had gotten him-self into. They said to take fifteen minutes, as they were gonna send so-and-so back to makeup and do a million other things. Mind you, this was years before everyone had cell phones or the internet, so we're just sitting around with nothing to do. They started calling us back to our places, as we were finally going to do it for real. We walk onstage, and all the camera guys are ready to go, but Paul wasn't there. We knew he had to be around, so we checked the vending machines and the fire escape, because we figured he might have ducked out for a cigarette. We came up empty, and it seemed that Paul had completely vanished.

Meanwhile, I'm just chatting with the camera crew and the band. We're all completely geared up to do this. Hell, I was only twenty at the time. This was huge! Fifteen minutes looking for Paul turned into thirty, at which point we're all saying, "Where the fuck is he?" His tour manager and manager hadn't seen him nor had any of the band. Everyone's getting paid, waiting to shoot this thing, and I'll never forget that Paul's manager at the time, said, "I can't believe I'm about to do this, but I'm going to call the hotel to see if he's there."

Gary comes back about three minutes later, looking like he'd seen a ghost. He said, "I called his room, and he answered." Paul had walked back to the hotel. Apparently, he thought there was too much commotion and bullshit, and he couldn't handle it. We're all standing there, thinking Gary and Paul might have been playing some really weird joke. Nope. Everyone from MTV starts looking at us, asking, "Where's your guy?" I stuttered, "Shit, he's not my guy!" I was at a loss for words and completely paralyzed. I felt like a total asshole in front of all these powerful people, with no answers. Finally, Gary had to say that Paul left because he didn't want to do it. At least he was honest about it.

We left, thinking, "Well, that's one way to completely burn a bridge with MTV forever." I was so bummed, but part of me was thinking, "Goddamn, what a punker." Paul never does things to be an asshole. For better or worse, he's taking care of himself and his principles. Even if it means letting a lot of people down, he was doing exactly what he felt like he needed to do. In the end, Paul didn't get his song in rotation. They weren't super keen on banging out his video that had just been released. The only thing that has survived from the whole fiasco is a clip of us playing "First Glimmer" that you can find online. It's actually really good, and it's because we didn't hear "lights, camera, action."

It's no secret that The Replacements had a permanent *Saturday Night Live* ban after they did the show in 1986. The funny thing was that *SNL* then booked Paul in 1993. I remember Lorne Michaels not realizing that it was Paul Westerberg from The Replacements until right after the show was done and then he was furious. We came in the day before the show to do a big, long rehearsal with the horn section. We were there all day, and the word was, "Everybody, don't talk too loud backstage about the fact that Paul was in The Replacements. Don't mention the 'R' word." Lorne still wanted his head on a stick. Basically, everyone backstage knew who Paul was, obviously, so it was really fun, with all of us playing dumb and mischievous for the day.

We got back the following day for another rehearsal, and there's a full run-through of the show in front of an audience around 8:00 p.m. We'd been there for fucking two straight days at that point, and Paul was getting antsy. We did "Knockin' On Mine" as our first song, which went fine. I think it was kinda nerve-wracking, even for Paul, because it's live, obviously. But it's also *SNL*. It's not exactly the club down the street. "Can't Hardly Wait" was our second song, and as we were walking to the stage, Paul whispered to me, "During one of the breaks, just yell something." He didn't tell me what to yell or why the drummer would be yelling some random thing on live TV. I think he just thought it would be funny or might piss off Lorne Michaels. Again, I'm a twenty-year-old kid, so no pressure, right?

I literally had no time to think up something that would be funny to yell, as we launched right into the song. It came to the first break in the song, and I choked. I didn't yell anything. To put this in perspective, this was a couple years before Burt Reynolds had his big resurgence in *Boogie Nights*. He was basically off the grid in terms of popularity in 1993. It was coming to the second break, and I'm thinking about Burt Reynolds. I was also thinking about Taco Bell's seven-layer-burrito, which had just come out around that time. I ended up yelling "Burt Reynolds!" at the top of my lungs. I wasn't mic'd, so if you were in the room, you definitely heard it, because I yelled. But if you were watching TV that night, you would have needed to hit rewind, thinking, "What the fuck did somebody just yell that made Westerberg crack up?"

The other funny thing was that Charlton Heston was hosting that night, and during rehearsals he kept screwing up Paul's last name. Poor Heston was so old and out of it at that time, and I have no idea what he would have been promoting in 1993. He was really struggling to remember Paul's last name, and it wasn't like he was being a jerk. He was just old, and we kinda felt bad for him. At the very end of the show, when everyone's on stage and the host thanks everyone, Paul was standing next to Heston. The way I remember it, Heston forgot the name again and doesn't even say, "Thanks to Paul Westerberg." I remember Heston pausing to say something to Paul, but he blanks and just stares at Paul like, "There's no fucking way I'm going to be able to remember your name again." Then he waved to the crowd and sticks his hand out to Paul, who coughs into his own hand right before they shake. If you ask Darren Hill, Paul's manager, he spit in his own hand before the shake, masking it with the cough.

That's what I love about Paul. I remember he turned down a big-money gig once because it wasn't about the money. He said, "Hey man, if I wanted to do it, I'd do it for free." I love that he's not filthy rich. Almost anybody else I know in his shoes would have jumped at the opportunity. If he doesn't feel right about it, he won't do it. I appreciate and admire that. I've also wanted to strangle him occasionally. I'll get pissed, and then he'll literally give me a big smooch, and we're buddies again. Paul can be a fucking bastard, but I love him, and I'll stick up for him until the end of time.

61

VIOLENT J/SHAGGY 2 DOPE

(Insane Clown Posse)

Whoop whoop! It feels fitting to end the book with ICP, perhaps the wildest, longest-enduring, and oddly endearing acts of the last three decades. Break out your hatchets and Faygo, fam, because here's Violent J and Shaggy 2 Dope on the craziest shit they've seen over the years.

Violent J: One time, when I lost my mind on stage, we were doing the song, "How Many Times." I had a microphone stand in front of me, my eyes were closed, and I was really feeling the song. I'm screaming and having my rock star moment. In my mind, I was Eddie Vedder, and I forgot for the moment that I was a fat clown. I was thinking the whole crowd was with me and totally feeling it. This was in Albuquerque, New Mexico, and there was stage-diving going on all night. When I finally opened my eyes, after doing this touching, emotional song, a kid was standing right in front of me. He was about two feet from my face, with his back to the crowd, facing me. He was flipping me off with two hands, the double birds, while looking right into my eyes.

I took my microphone stand, swung it like a battle axe, and split the top of his head open. The crowd went silent and then started cheering after a three-second shock. I went on with the show like nothing had happened. After the show, when I got backstage, I was covered in Faygo and soaking wet. The cops were waiting there to arrest me, and they took me down to the police station. They had four witnesses sitting there, and they all had clown paint on. I'm looking at them like, "You motherfuckers! You're painted like me and snitching me out!" It was hella fucked up, and we ended up getting banned from Albuquerque for seven years.

Years later, whenever we were playing somewhere in the Southwest, a huge posse of 200 juggalos from Albuquerque would show up and chant, "505! 505!" That was the Albuquerque area code, so they would always let us know they were in the house. They did that for years, and when we were finally allowed back into Albuquerque, we got a hero's return. The kid I hit ended up suing me, and I had to pay him $30,000. I was walking to the tour bus one day, and a guy literally jumped out of the bushes to serve me papers. He said, "Joe Bruce?" I thought he was asking for an autograph. That's the last time I did anything like that because it was before I learned that if you beat someone's ass, you get sued.

Shaggy 2 Dope: The shittiest thing that happened to me was at one of the Gatherings, sometime around 2006. Our dumb asses would wrestle during the day before going on stage. We had wrestled these two big cowboy dudes, and I hyperextended my knee. I thought I broke it, but I snapped my ACL in half. The show had to go on, so we go on stage, we're turning it out, and my dumb ass decides to climb the lighting rig. That thing was stupid high, and I decided to climb it halfway, with my knee all fucked up, and do a back flip into the crowd. I get up there, go to do the flip, and my knee gave out. I ended up doing a ridiculous-looking back dive, and I must have been about twenty-five feet in the air.

I didn't realize what had actually happened until I was being hoisted back on stage. I blacked out, and I feel bad thinking about the people I must have crunched. I hope that I just straight hit the ground, because if I clocked someone else's head, that'd be like getting hit with a fucking cannonball. They threw me back on stage, and I was basically unconscious on my feet. I ended up finishing the show, and after limping backstage, I started puking blood.

I didn't do anything about it and just bounced home. The next day, my left arm wasn't working. I'm the kind of guy that when something is fucked up, I just assume the human body can heal anything. Now I go right to the fucking doctor, but back then, I thought I was indestructible. Two months went by, and I couldn't turn my head to the left and couldn't sleep on my side. Finally, my boy said, "You look like a fucking idiot. You gotta go to the doctor." I fought tooth and nail, but right after the doctor X-rayed me, he said, "Holy shit. We need to get you into surgery right now." I had shattered two of my discs, and the reason my arm didn't work was because a shard from one of the discs was poking into my spinal cord. The weird part was that my hand worked fine, but my arm just flopped around. I could still rap shit, but it looked like I had a rubber arm on stage. To this day, my shit's fucked up. I had broken my neck previous to that wrestling, and I let that one heal on its own. I'm not paralyzed, but I play it off real good.

Violent J: The scariest fan interaction I've had was when we played New York City. We got in the bus after the show and drove out of the city at night. After a few hours, we stopped at a Denny's and were inside having a late-night, early morning breakfast. Suddenly, our bus driver said, "What the fuck is that?" He pointed out to the parking lot, and we could see a kid standing on top of the bus. He was in the process of climbing down when we all ran out there. He had gotten up on the bus sometime during our show in NYC and hung on the entire time on the road. This fucking kid rode on the roof through tunnels and highways all the way out of the city. He could have been fucking knocked off, or fallen, at any time.

We could see that he had been so scared that he had pissed himself up there. We had been driving for about two hours, so who knows what would have happened if we hadn't stopped. We used to roll with this guy Tom Dub at the time, who was this skinny-ass, frail kid. I don't know why he did it, but Tom Dub straight cold-cocked the kid. Tom was so weak that his fist just bounced off the kid's face. The kid looked at Tom Dub like, "What the fuck?" and then he walked away like David Banner, with pissed pants.

Shaggy 2 Dope: Here's a good story about how I got my first Rolex. We were on our Wicked Clowns from Outer Space Tour, and it was so fucking long that we started going a little bit crazy. We were out for two or three months at a time, and it wasn't some cushy Taylor Swift or Justin Bieber tour. We were basically living in a minivan and starting to go fucking batty. One day, we pulled into some small town in the Midwest, and there was a little river running through town. We pulled up to it and said, "What can we do to get fucking paid right now?" We decided to hold the van for ransom. We found a board and a brick, put the brick on the gas, and the board between the brick and the gas, to hold it in place.

It was revving, and all we had to do was slam it into drive. We called our manager and said, "We're about to drive this fucking van into a river. What do we get if we don't?" I can't remember what J asked for, but I said, "I want a Rolex." He said, "Done." We didn't crash the van into the river because our demands were met. Our manager just didn't want the hassle of dealing with it, and we would have probably ended up in jail. I don't think you can purposely drive a van into a downtown river without going to jail, especially if you're a clown.

Violent J: I don't want to sound like a brutalizer of our fans, but this one happened when we were playing the third annual Gathering of the Juggalos. Back then, the fans used to storm the stage. They'd stage dive back down, but when more and more started rushing the stage, the stage got flooded and they stopped diving. After the show was over, they'd tear down the stage and smash up our set. I don't wear much jewelry, but I do wear a diamond Hatchet Man, which is our logo, around my neck. When the fans stormed the stage, I noticed a kid eyeing my Hatchet Man. I pulled it off my neck, and stuck it in my pocket.

There were about 200 people on stage, so we were all smooshed together. The kid stuck his hand in my pocket, snatched my chain, and jumped off the front of the stage. I was on him, man. I smashed through the crowd with all my weight, dove off the stage, and landed right on top of him. I still had my cordless microphone in my hand, and I started bashing the kid in the head. I was trying to dig my chain out of his fist, which he was clenching really tight. I kept bashing him until his hand slowly opened up, and I got my necklace back.

I was totally winded at this point, but I pushed my way through the crowd, climbed over the barricade, and got backstage. I laid on my back, catching my wind, but the whole time I was thinking, "I gotta get the fuck outta here. I probably just killed that kid." I yelled, "Get me outta here," and my friends helped me up. They threw me in the van, and we floored it out of there. This Gathering was in Toledo, and on our way home, I saw a pond on the side of the road. We pulled off the exit, and I threw the microphone in the pond because I thought I had a murder weapon on my hands. Before I chucked it, I looked at the mic, and the end of it was totally flat from bashing that kid in the head. A microphone is basically a steel ball, so I really fucked that kid up.

When I got home, I called my manager and said, "After you cleared everyone out, was a kid laying there dead?" He said no, so I asked, "Nobody was injured?" He said, "No, what are you talking about?" I said, "Nothing, don't worry about it" and hung up.

ACKNOWLEDGMENTS

This book wouldn't exist without the artists who generously gave me their time and a little piece of their souls. I also want to thank all the publicists and managers who fought for me and whom I nearly bugged to death throughout this process. David and Jacob for taking a chance on me. Rob Elder for being the best mentor a guy could have. All my friends. All my family. All in my heart forever.

ABOUT THE AUTHOR

Drew Fortune is a pop-culture journalist and screenwriter, who has been actively publishing for the past ten years. He is a regular contributor to *Vanity Fair, Rolling Stone, Esquire*, and *Vulture*, but his writings on music, film, and television have been published in *Cosmopolitan, Playboy, SPIN, Billboard*, the *A.V. Club, Stereogum*, and many others. His favorite bands are Ween, Superchunk, and The Replacements. He loves fly fishing and loitering in record stores.